How to Manage Your Manager
All the Credit, Half the Work

Milo Denison

Copyright © 2018 Milo Denison

All rights reserved.

ISBN:
978-1-7324479-2-9

Chapters

1. Introduction
2. Why This Book?
3. Kiss Ass (Playing the Game)
4. Self-Promote
5. Become an Extrovert
6. Know the Books
7. Dumb it Down
8. Get Others on Your Side
9. Use the Slang
10. Yes, and…
11. Customer Service of Everything
12. Bad Managers
13. Good Managers
14. When You Have Too Many Bosses
15. Inside the Box
16. Backstabbing
17. At the End of the Week
18. Bonus Chapter: Office Pranks
19. Appendix

ACKNOWLEDGMENTS

I would like to thank all the friends I have made over the years in the corporate world. If it weren't for you, my years behind the desk would not have been as enjoyable as they were. And, of course, I wouldn't have been inspired to write this book.

Introduction

A long, long time ago, more specifically in the year 1998, I started working as a customer service agent at a telephone company call center. My role was simple, come in on time, log in, answer questions as they arrive, take a break at the allotted break time, and go home. Every minute of my time throughout the day was tracked. If I logged out for a break too early or logged in too late, or if I took more than the allotted exceptions, my manager would have a talk with me. If I exceeded my average handle time with a customer too often, my manager would have a talk with me. If my average hold time was too long, my manager would have a talk with me. If I did anything outside of the clearly documented list of policies, my manager would have a talk with me. If my manager had too many talks with me, I would receive a write up and other disciplinary actions. At first, I played along with the game, being very happy when my average handle times (AHT) were some of the lowest on the team. I would relish the rewards they put in place for those, like myself, who exceeded all the defined goals of call times, handle times, and other KPIs (key performance indicators). However, I found the rewards I received for being a top performer didn't equate to the amount of time and energy I was putting into being one.

It was at that call center I met Brendan. He had been with the company a year or so longer than me, and so he received the premium choice of desks in our team area—next to the window. Brendan and I would stand and toss foam balls back and forth while explaining to our customers how to calculate a prorated invoice. We would head out after work for drinks at Canyons, the local bar, for the phone grunts that we were. And we would occasionally carpool to work, knowing that we both had to be logged into the IVR (interactive voice response) within two minutes of our scheduled start time.

Brendan also became my first mentor in the corporate world. I didn't think of him as a mentor, to me he was just a good friend showing me the ropes. Prior to that it was a long list of jobs from pizza delivery driver, to walking lab samples from one department to another in a hospital. They were all jobs that I took too seriously, causing frustration and conflict on my part. It was in the corporate world, as a call center employee, that I learned a valuable lesson, one that Brendan taught me, a lesson of trying to get away with as much as I could whenever possible. He got me started on a long road of learning to work the system while working within the system. If a company is going to monitor every move a person makes, and everything a person says, we should at least have a little fun trying to get away with as much as possible—a bit like high school.

"Whenever there is a chance to sign up for team incentives, do it." He told me one day as we were logged out of our telephony systems. "Hey Andy," he said to one of the other team managers as we walked up. "You guys interested in having a contest with our team to see who has the best call times?" After Andy agreed, we walked to the next manager repeating this process as slowly as possible. With each team manager, we might challenge them to average call times, or average time in Aux. The metric wasn't important, and it usually involved the losing team providing a potluck lunch for both teams. What mattered was the time we spent headset free, not having to listen to customers complain about the lack of coverage our wireless phone company offered, or the roaming charges. This was in the late 90s, before the era of national calling.

"Another good one is decorating the team area for holidays. Not only do you get to take time to do the decorating, you have to get the decorations." This one he told me while we were cutting turkey and other thanksgiving themed items out of paper, and taping them around all the desks.

What Brendan taught a young man (me), who previously believed in working hard, doing your best, and going above and beyond whenever possible, is that being an over-achiever only irritates people. He taught me that a person can be just as successful in life cutting corners, as those who work hard and overachieve. These were all valuable lessons I carried with me throughout the rest of my career.

In the business aisle of most bookstores—assuming there is still a bookstore where you live—you will find plenty of publications written by "professionals" with a long list of credentials next their names. The books written by these experts are usually on the subject of how to be a good manager and leader. They offer advice on how to hire the best people, and how to get the best out of those who work in the organization. Most noticeably, the books are how-to guides on inspiring others and moving ahead within a company. Occasionally, a book on the subject of managing your manager is slipped in as well. These books often explain how to move ahead within a company, they just have a different title and list of credentials next to the authors' name.

I don't have a problem with those books as a whole. Most actually do include some useful advice for being successful in the corporate environment, and offer good advice on how to work well with others. All of which is intended to help people achieve corporate success. I guess my problem with a lot of those books, that I hope to address in this one, is they take themselves too seriously. The authors try to come off as experts on the subject of working in a corporate environment, generally glossing over the comedy of errors that is the corporate world. This book is about those errors, it is about the lessons learned from someone who has done the job both well and poorly. The experts (the ones who have actually worked in business) write the books, implying that they were great at working with their manager, and since they were so good at it they wrote a book to teach everyone else how to do the same. This book, however, describes a bit about how great I was in the corporate environment, and a lot about how I was not-so-great in the corporate environment.

For every manager in a company, there is a group of people who work for him or her. The average manager will usually have eight to ten direct reports;[i] not all are looking to become the next boss, but most are looking to be successful in their job. Many people simply work with the intent of making a decent income and enjoying life from that income. They are not necessarily interested in telling others how to do their job. Those who fall into that category look to provide their families with a decent home, a regular vacation, and maybe pay a bit of their children's college education. To provide this financial stability doesn't necessarily involve climbing the corporate ladder to a leadership position. But it does involve earning a decent amount of money through annual pay raises, and through staying employed over the long term.

Successfully managing your managers does not involve telling your bosses what you actually think of them, it doesn't involve coming in late, taking excessive coffee breaks, and generally doing as little as possible. Yet, if you are the person who comes in late and does as little as possible, you still need to convince those around you that you are showing up on time and going above and beyond the call of duty. You convince your managers, and others, that you are a top performer while doing less, by being the one who decorates the team area with turkeys.

The corporate ladder is a misnomer in my opinion. The corporate world equates to a pyramid more than a ladder. The larger base of employees is what supports the top of the pyramid, which is known as the CEO and executive board. The CEO (chief executive officer) is the tip of the pyramid, which then flows down to the mass grouping of employees at the bottom known as the rest of us.

So, where are all the books on how to be a good employee, and how to be successful while not working your way to the top? I've done some searching and I was able to find a few books and articles on the subject of being a good employee, and getting your manager to work for you. Many of those books have similar titles to this one. But for the most part no one writes those books, because we have been taught to always be moving ahead in the corporate world. Annual evaluations and reviews usually involve a conversation about where to next. And if you were to tell a peer you are happy where you are, they might look at you as if something is wrong with you.

I once worked with a guy who was happy in his role as a call center representative, answering customers' questions all day long. He always received the schedule he wanted, since he been with the company for so long; it usually involved four 10-hour shifts and three days off. He was good at his job, always getting high ratings for customer satisfaction, and he viewed the job as low stress. Come in, do the job, go home and enjoy the rest of life. Yet when asked where he wanted to go next, and he said he was fine where he was, people looked at him as though there was something wrong with him. He didn't want to move ahead, he was happy and content where he was.

I would hazard a guess from my time in the corporate world, for every person who views a management role as something to achieve, there is another person who views management positions as something to be avoided. The avoiders often look at management as more stress and work that they don't want. Yet, we are taught that success involves moving up.

Outside of the office, we discuss what we do for a living, often bragging to our friends about the number of people we manage, as if it makes us more important. We talk about the difficult workload we have, implying that we are the only ones who do the job as well as we do it. We show off the cars we buy, and other tangible items, so that people can see our success. We want to make the big bucks because we want to get the biggest house with the biggest TV, and gain the envy and respect of our peers.

(House sq ft/Job Title)Salary = Success

So, what do we need to do in order to achieve this success? Should we buy the books and watch the videos on being a successful leader, on moving up in the corporation, and everything else that is pitched to us on the subject? We could if that is what we want. At various points in my life, that is what I wanted. I wanted to manage a coffee shop when I was in the coffee business, I wanted to manage a team when I was in the software business, and even now I manage people in the photography and film business. Sometimes I will buy those books in order to improve my ability to motivate people. Other times I don't want to be a manager. Sometimes I just want to go in on a given day and blankly stare at my computer monitor for the first few hours. What I don't want, is for others to know that what I am doing for the first few hours of my day, is listening to *Portishead* while blankly staring at the trees outside the window.

Let's be real, most of us are employees, and most of us are going to stay employees. Sorry to burst your bubble and your dreams of winning the corner office, along with your dreams of winning the lottery each week. Even as we work our way up the corporate pyramid, there will usually still be someone above us who gets to tell us what to do. That person has the better office, bigger house, and fancier car. Remember the 1%? The 1% is the top of the pyramid, the rest of it is the rest of us. We are the people who come in each day and do the actual work that makes the managers and executives look good. It is us that make the leaders great leaders, and we make the companies that we work for bigger and more valuable. We might move up to a leadership position or we might not. Some of us want to move up and some of us don't.

In life, not everyone should be in a management position. Maybe the current manager knew the right person or played golf with the right executive. Maybe they have the degree that makes it seem as though they know what they are doing, but really only proves that they were able to sit in a room, and retain information long enough to pass a test at the end of the term. For every great manager, there are twice as many mediocre or even bad ones. Good and bad managers need great employees, because without great employees everyone fails. For small companies, this could mean going out of business. For large companies, this could mean the team being made redundant and laid off, just because a single bad manager didn't make the team look good. Is it all the bad managers' fault? Perhaps it is. But some of the fault is also ours for not taking the initiative and managing that manager in a way that gets the best out of them. It doesn't really matter in the end how that manager reached their position within the company. What matters is that they are there. They might only be there for a short time, or they might not move into another role for a very long time. You might only work for that person for a few weeks, or months, or you might be working with that person for years. In any amount of time it is your responsibility to be as successful as possible, even if you are only in the chair for the paycheck.

Some managers truly do know what they are doing, and deserve to be in that position. These are the ones we want to work for, the ones that require less work on our part. I've worked for good people and it is rewarding to know that the person is there for me and wants me to succeed. As with each good manager, I could name one who was just the opposite. I could tell stories, and I will tell a few of them in this book, about the ones who would throw me under the bus in order to make him or her look good. I have worked for people who could not care less about my success in an organization, and were only focused on themselves. I will also relay a few stories of the great managers who worked just as hard for my success as I did for theirs.

How to Manage Your Manager asks the question, how do we make our manager, good or bad, believe that we are the best employee without actually having to be the best employee? This book is also about influencing that person to implement initiatives in the corporate world, that should be implemented instead of their own ideas. This can be done in some situations, but in others it is best to let your brilliant idea lie, and wait for another opportunity. Managing your manager is about knowing when to push something, and when to let it drop. It is about influencing through personality and creativity. *How to Manage Your Manager* is part successful laziness, and part working efficiently, all the while gaining as much credit as possible.

This book is written from the point of view of how to be successful in a corporate environment. The larger the corporation, the more relevant the information contained in this book. The larger the company, the easier it is for someone to get lost in the crowd. As a company grows, its ability to evolve with a changing market diminishes. People who have worked for the company a long time become set in their ways; they figure that is what worked in the past and made them a success will continue to work going forward. Smaller companies are often more agile, and better able to see the faults in bad people and remove them. Smaller companies such as startups have the ability to be more nimble, as they haven't developed this rigidity yet. When they are working on an issue they don't have defined processes, policies, and existing ways of doing business in place. The staff have a closer working relationship with one another. Larger companies, however, create a work environment that distances people from one another. Large corporations have established policies and procedures to deal with most situations. If something comes up that is not guided by a policy, they will create one for the next time. They will have checks and balances, and a list of priorities that is associated with a list of people who must sign off on it before it can move forward. Many large companies will unintentionally create silos that put one team over here, and another team over there; rarely do the two teams ever talk to one another, only looking at the job from a single point of view. This doesn't mean that a startup is a better place to work; statistically speaking most startups go out of business. [ii] Startups come and go, people move around a lot, and there is a lot of sudden change in the startup world. In addition, if it is a good business or product, the startup might be bought out by a larger company, bringing many of the employees into the larger corporate fold. The idea of looking like you do more while doing less doesn't apply, because most starting businesses require everyone involved to be one hundred percent behind the product. This involves drinking the Kool-Aid from morning until well into the night.

If a company has been around long enough to have thousands of employees, they must have done something right at some point. But these larger environments can be a challenging place to work in, especially because, as they hire more and more people, the human resources department and the hiring manager have less time to focus on individual skills, and instead start looking for specific degrees and keywords embedded in applicant resumes to speed up the hiring process. They might look for past experience with other well-known companies. It's less about the person and more about the piece of paper. With larger multinational companies, sometimes it is simply about getting the bodies into seats. Unfortunately, once they are in, it is harder to get them out, and once they are in, if they play the corporate game right they will move ahead, they will succeed, and yet they might not be the most deserving person. That person could be you. You might not be the most qualified person for the role, you might not be the best person for the role, or you might be the greatest employee that the company has ever had. It doesn't really matter, what matters is that your manager and your manager's manager think you are the greatest employee ever.

Please be aware that all situations and examples described in this book are actual events. I did, however, change the names of the people involved, and left out some details in order to protect the privacy of the people I am referencing, and of course not to piss anyone off and have them contact me bitching about what I wrote.

Why This Book?

First, let us start off with why you should not read this book. That is a much easier question to answer than why you should read it. As you can see on the cover by the lack of credentials next to my name, I am not an expert sociologist or, for that matter, an expert in any field really—although I would consider myself relatively knowledgeable in a variety of areas. I don't have an advanced degree; I didn't spend years in research institutes interviewing people in the corporate environment. I haven't spent hours talking to managers and employees in an attempt to understand the business world, and what makes them successful. I'm not super rich, and I have no name recognition. Instead, my knowledge comes from twenty plus years of my life working for some of the largest software and technology companies in the world. Before working in an office environment with those companies, I worked for coffee shops, construction companies, print shops, and I have subsequently spent the remainder of my time working as a photographer, indie-filmmaker, and author of books like this. Does twenty years in the corporate world give me the expertise to write a book on working in a corporate environment, compared to someone who has just studied corporate culture? Perhaps. I would respond with another question. If you were on a sailboat in the Pacific Ocean, would you prefer to have someone there who has spent twenty years as a sailor, or someone who has simply studied the subject of sailing?

Another reason you should consider not buying this book is that it might offend you. My last book, *"An Expat's Guide to Ireland: Life in a Second World Country"* enraged a few Irish people to the point that I could see their desire to punch me upon hearing the title. Of course, they didn't read it to find out what I really thought, but as we all know, a single sentence can offend easily. Irish people take a lot of pride in their country, so when someone refers to it as a second world country, they might take offense. And of course, people might find it irritating at my incorrect use of the term second world.

Based on a lifetime of interactions with people, it wouldn't surprise me if this book might also contain at least one sentence that could offend. The introduction you just read could come across as if I am opposed to the corporate lifestyle. It might seem like I am against large corporations, but to be clear, I am not. A large corporation provided me with a good stable income for a long time, it also moved me to another country, and provided me with a lot of life experiences. Most importantly, a large corporation gave me the inspiration to write this book. It happened one day when a manager of mine made a statement, about how it seemed I was managing him more than he was managing me.

If you are someone who is in a management position, you might be looking through this book thinking that I am trying to give advice on how to get one over on you. You especially might find it offensive, because some of the advice contained within it is actually on that subject. But don't be offended, because this book is also for you. Having been in management myself, I know the balance one should try to create in order to be a good manager for one's employees, while also looking towards the larger goals that the company has in place. Yet there was always someone in a position of authority over me that I reported to, just like there is for you. Learning to work with that person successfully, and getting them to work on my behalf, was just as important as the relationship with the people who worked for me.

I've felt the frustration and aggravation from working with a bad manager who should never have been allowed to manage others. I have also felt the sense of self-worth that comes from working for an inspiring leader. Across the board, managing my manager hasn't been something to be ignored. With each role, whether working for a good or bad manager, I have been just as responsible for my successes or failures as the person I worked for. Over the years, I have learned through working with, and for, so many people, that dealing correctly with the person I report to, will pay off in both financial rewards and job satisfaction.

Another good reason not to buy this book is that it might not actually contain any useful information for you. Personally, I find that hard to believe, but I guess it is possible. I spent many years of my life learning how to be unsuccessful, yes unsuccessful, in a corporate environment. I gained years of experience that I have passed on to those I have mentored, and can now write down and pass on to others. I even did a little research for this book, talking to others and reading a few of those books I made fun of in the introduction to this one.

What will you get out of reading this book, and why should you read it? Hopefully you will gain knowledge, insight, and a more relaxed work life. The worst outcome of not effectively managing your manager affects personal happiness. By not successfully managing your manager, you might dread coming to work each day, and anxiously leave at the end of the day, mentally exhausted. Throughout this book, I will provide real world examples from my own experience, as well as those relayed to me by others. As a reader of this who might find yourself becoming frustrated in the day-to-day repetition of your work environment, hopefully you can take some of this knowledge, and use it to be more successful in managing your own manager. You might view success differently to others, you might view it as doing less for more, or you might view it as getting rewarded for the work you do, and have not been receiving. It doesn't matter how you view success, by effectively managing the person who is managing you, you will move closer to achieving that success. Studies by academics with no real-world experience can be helpful, but someone who has lived and worked in the trenches of the workforce from retail to cushy office job can speak from real world experience.

From the age that I was old enough to get that first paper route to the point in life that I left my cushy well paid corporate job, there has always been someone that I answered too. Over all those years, I made more mistakes in my interactions than accomplishments. It has been said that we learn more from our mistakes than we do from the successes and with that, the reason you should continue reading this book is you would be learning from someone who has made many good and bad decisions over the years in the way he interacts with his employer.

If you have a good working relationship with your manager, you might laugh at work on occasion, you might receive positive treatment from your boss, and instead of walking into the office with dread and anxiety, you might actually look forward to going to work each day. This will have an impact on raises and reviews, and as we all know, money doesn't necessarily buy happiness, but it sure does buy things that make us happy—like exotic vacations and hookers.

Kiss Ass (Playing the Game)

Yes, everyone says that they are not ass-kissers, but believe me, the successful employees who get good raises and promotions are. And be honest with yourself-in a way, we are all ass-kissers. We might not think so, we might think we stand up for our opinions or beliefs, but do we really? Think about the times when you were sitting in a meeting and the big boss had a terrible idea. You thought to yourself how terrible it was, and how it would not work. Did you say something? Is that not ass-kissing in a way? Sure, you didn't tell them the idea was brilliant, and you didn't bring an apple to set it on the boss's desk, but you also were not calling out their bullshit. Ass-kissing isn't just about brown-nosing, it is also about telling the boss, or the bosses what they want to hear. The person in the room who gets to hear what they want is the HIPPO (The highest paid person's opinion). If you want to be on their bad side, then point out the flaws of their idea. The best place to point out those flaws is in the conference room with people around. Don't want to do that? Well then you are kissing a bit of HIPPO butt.

By deciding to sit quietly, thinking to yourself how the idea will fail, and doing nothing about it, you might not be kissing ass, but you aren't doing anything that is going to make you look good in the company either. Instead of sitting and doing nothing, tell them what a good idea it is. You know what else managers love, it is if you ask follow-up questions to the proposal or presentation, because you 'care' so much about that idea you want to know more. If it makes you feel better, don't think if it as kissing ass, think of it as playing the corporate game. The game where your goal is to end up with more cards than anyone else in the room, and the HIPPO is the dealer who hands out those cards.

    I used to work with this guy, who we will call Eric. Eric was-and still is-a very good friend of mine, so I say this with the utmost respect: he is one of the best ass-kissers in a corporate environment I have ever known. It isn't that he actually kisses ass, instead, what he does is he plays the game. He knows who to be friends with, and whose lame ideas to support. Over the years that Eric and I worked together, we shared the same manager three times in three separate roles. Eric might disagree with this, but I know I did more actual work than he did, however, I didn't play the game as well as he did. Just the opposite, I was the guy who stood up for my opinions, talked back, informed people when they were doing something wrong, and didn't back down because I knew I was morally and logically right, which usually I was. Remember that HIPPO with the terrible idea? Most people sat in the conference room thinking it was a bad idea, Eric agreed with the HIPPO saying it was a great idea, while I alone voiced an opposing opinion.

But I was also the low man in the pyramid, and as such, no matter how right I was, there was someone with more authority than me to tell me I was wrong, and to stop questioning the boss. It took me many years to figure out that when I whenever I spoke up in those meetings, the only outcome was that I would be the guy the bosses didn't want to deal with the guy they did not want to promote or move up in the company. Eric, being the agreeable one, was the one who got the promotions. Even when after a few months, when the project that the HIPPO came up with had failed; I never got a, "you were right Milo, it didn't work." That project would simply move from an active status to a closed status on a spreadsheet, a new project would come along, and the cycle would repeat.

Eric played the game by the rules defined within the hierarchy of the corporate world. I am not saying he didn't work or stand up for himself, I am saying he did the right work, the work that made him look good, and when it came to raises and promotions, he quickly moved above me. The reason he was promoted over me was because I didn't say what the powers in charge wanted to hear. In the corporate world, do as Eric does, not as Milo does.

When it came to being successful and kissing ass, Eric went along with projects and initiatives, even when he knew they wouldn't work out. The reason he went along with these ideas is because he was aware that fighting against the project would be detrimental to his career. He followed the advice listed at the beginning of this chapter. Instead of sitting quietly and not saying anything, he went along with the idea. He made it clear to the HIPPO that he liked the idea, so the HIPPO would ask him to be involved in the project. Later on, the idea might fail, or it might have been canceled, but he would still get the credit for participating in it, and for supporting the HIPPO. He could still show his good work, and how he supported the person in charge as best as he could.

Another way that Eric was successful, was by becoming friends with the decision makers in the company. He would chat socially with his bosses, and occasionally hang out for a beer outside of work if that was an option. Eric practiced the techniques outlined in *"How to Win Friends and Influence People,"*[iii] without ever having read the book. Personally, I would argue that the advice listed in the book is outdated, and the modern world doesn't work like it did in 1937 when the book was originally published. We can see this in the successful election of our 45th President of the United States, someone who wrote a book that is the complete opposite of *"How to Win Friends and Influence People."*

I don't know exactly what Eric earns now but I do know it is more than I do. I know during my time in the corporate world he earned more than I did at every step, even though we both started at the same wage. And I know now that he has a pretty sweet corporate role, because he did what I'm telling you to do. If you have morals that you want to stand up for, get a job for a non-profit and spend your time in the cold with a sign in your hands in front of the capitol building. If you want to be successful, check those morals at the door. I've often joked that when I went from being the pariah in the office to becoming successful in the corporate world, it was when I began checking my soul at the door. At one point I had to change companies, since I had burned so many bridges at the old one. But in the new company, I made sure to follow the lead that I had learned from people like Eric. By checking my morals at the door, I eventually began to find success in the corporate world, receiving accolades for work completed, and for my dealings with others.

For the people reading this, thinking that they don't work in a corporate environment, this can apply to all work environments, not just the corporate one. Many years ago, I worked for a large well-known international coffee company. In that role, I was a supervisor, and took my job way too seriously. I was also young enough at the time to still have morals about how people should be treated by others. Remember as children how we are taught that people should be treated as equals, and to treat others as you want them to treat you? That is good advice to give our children, but to be successful in life, it is not wise to follow that policy, especially in the United States, where customers have become accustomed to a certain type of service. To become a large, successful, retail outlet like this coffee company, they needed to follow the "customer is always right" policy, which does not work well alongside the "treat others as equals" philosophy. Since this was a large corporate coffee chain, the rules were set at the top, and flowed downstream with no question. The customer is always right. End of discussion.

For example, on one occasion, a customer leaned over the counter too far while a barista was steaming milk, and some splashed on his suit jacket. Or at least he said it did. That customer then complained about the splashed milk. Firstly, I couldn't even see any on his gray jacket, tie, or anywhere else on the guy. Secondly, even if any did splash on his jacket, and I don't think it did, it would have been his fault for leaning over the counter like a dumbass. That is part of the reason the counters and back splashes are there—to keep the customer at a safe distance from the preparation area. At the time, it was our Sunday crowd. This was the post church crowd who would often visit the location, so we were a little busy, and my patience with the customer was low. I also felt a moral obligation, as the supervisor, to stick up for the barista, who was being yelled at by him. Figuring he was just fishing for a free drink, I gave him a free drink certificate, and sent him on his way, not really thinking much about it after that.

As often happens with people who don't get what they really want, he went above me and complained to my district manager. It turned out that what he wanted was for his suit to be cleaned free of charge. As my father would say, it was "mighty Christian of him," implying not very Christian at all for someone who had just left church. My district manager paid for his suit to be cleaned—the full suit, not just the jacket. She then proceeded, along with my manager, to reprimand me for being dismissive to him, and apparently rude. Truthfully, I probably was rude to him, having little patience for people like that. She also told me the story about how, once, a customer threw a cup at her and she responded with, "I can't help you if you are going to throw things at me." Personally, I would have thrown something back at the person, because I believe in the "treat others as they have already treated you" rule.

What does this have to do with kissing ass and telling them what they want to hear? Well, that is the next part of the story. As I was getting chewed out for my lack of kindness to our high maintenance customers, I was also waiting on a transfer to another location. I had moved apartments and wanted to work within walking distance of my new apartment. There was another location in the chain, and making coffee at one location is the same as making coffee at another. But since they didn't feel that I was nice to people, they wouldn't approve my transfer until I had proven that I could be nice to the customers. I said fine and went back to work. Knowing that I needed to play along in order to get my transfer, but still feeling I was in the right, I didn't change my interactions with customers that much. I talked and socialized with the regulars I liked, and still looked down upon the high maintenance ones I deplored. To my manager, however, I acted all happy and awesome, especially when she was around. At one point, I literally said the words, "This whole being nice to customers isn't that hard". Which of course she bought into, and a few weeks later approved my transfer to the other location. Not because I had actually changed anything, but because I pretended to buy in to the attitude of my manager. The attitude of great customer service at all costs: kissing ass.

The moral of the story is, kiss ass if you want to move ahead and get what you want. I didn't want a promotion, I just wanted a simple store transfer. And how did I get it? I pretended to care about what they wanted. Kiss your customer's ass, kiss your boss's ass, and kiss every ass that your boss kisses. Just pick one cheek while your boss kisses the other, and occasionally move over to the boss's ass and give that some loving as well so that it doesn't feel neglected. And don't worry, as you move up the chain you will eventually start getting someone right up your ass too, creating a loving corporate style human centipede of ass kissing.

Okay, maybe the human centipede reference is a bit overboard but you get the point. Don't be a blatant ass kisser by telling your manager they look good, or by bringing them coffee each morning. Kiss ass and play the game by backing them up in a meeting when they throw out a proposal that sucks, and tell them it is a great idea. If they ask a question, always respond with, "That's a good question." When they ask for volunteers, raise your hand and volunteer—even if you have no intention of doing the work or just plan to pass it off to someone else. They love to see that initiative. If they take the wrong side of a debate, or feel the customer is right when they are not, agree with them.

If you have a hard time with the idea of using the term ass-kissing, think of it like a date. This will make it a little more fun and less soul destroying. Remember that date you were on with that person who was telling you a boring story, and you spaced off, but then paid attention again to laugh at the funny part? That is what it is like when you are in a planning meeting, where your bosses are going through a PowerPoint presentation on the goals for the next fiscal year and targets that need to be met. It is all information that really doesn't affect what you do on a daily basis, so you space off and occasionally nod your head when they look around the room, as if you were listening and agree with what they are saying. You smile and tell them it is great. Your goal on the boring date is to get something from the hot person sitting across the table from you at the end of the night. Your goal when pretending to care about next year's growth forecast and the new company motto, is to go back to your desk and check how much your 401K plan has grown as you work your way closer to retirement.

Self-Promote

The art of self-promotion begins from the day that you are hired, through to the day you are fired— or you quit. Think about it like this, during the interview you tell the company why they should hire you over everyone else they are interviewing. The first conversation you have with your potential new boss involves promoting yourself. Since the first series of discussions you have with your new employer is essentially self-promotion, why should it suddenly end the day you receive the offer letter and sit down at a new desk, with its ergonomic keyboard and glare-reducing monitor?

During the interview, if they ask how well you work with others do you respond with, "I'd prefer not to work with others at all since most people are idiots." No, you tell them about your great communication skills, since good communication skills are the number one thing most employers are looking for when hiring new employees. [iv] When the interviewer asks about your weaknesses, you don't respond with "Gin and tonic", you tell them that you have a tendency to work late, and need to try not to work so much. The whole interview process involves speaking highly of yourself, explaining how you are absolutely the best qualified candidate for the job. The same level of self-promotion is the method of communication you need to use in every one-on-one you have with your manager, with your manager's manager, your peers, and everyone else you interact with on any given day. Pretending that every day is an interview will go further than behaving like the know-it-all employee who has been there forever.

Look at the person across the table doing the interview. When asked how they like working for the company, they don't respond with, "I'm just waiting until retirement or death, whichever happens first." No, they respond with, "It's a great company to work for. Yes, the hours can be long sometimes, but it is totally worth it because they treat the employees so well here." Everyone knows both sides of the interview are BS, but we do it anyway because the interviewee is promoting his or herself, while the interviewer is promoting the company.

As children, we are told that if we work hard we will be recognized for it and it will pay off. The reality is this never happens. Okay, maybe 'never' is too strong of a statement. Let's just say that it rarely happens. That is something we figure out much later in life, when the reality of the world has set in, and we find out that working hard is only a portion of being successful. And in some cases, with some companies, hard work is only a small portion of success. You can actually work hard and tell your manager on a regular basis how hard you are working, or you can work not as hard, and still tell your manager how hard you are working. What sounds better: doing more work and getting credit for it, or doing less work and getting the same amount of credit? You can be the one to decide on that, but no matter which choice you make, letting others know about the great work you do is the key.

One of the misconceptions of dealing with managers is that we assume our manager knows what we do each day. We assume it is their responsibility to keep up to date on the projects we have completed, and to know how great we are without telling them. But think about it from their point of view. They are managing multiple people, and even though you might meet with them regularly, you can't expect them to remember what you did last week, or last month, that was so great in comparison to any other person in your work group. Think about the most successful thing you did at work three months ago? Not easy to remember, is it? Now look at the people sitting around you, and think about what each of them did three months ago. Sure, it´s not your job to know that, but even if it were your job, how hard would it be to do so?

At your annual review should you expect your manager to then remember all the great things you did over the past year out of everyone else that works for them? Of course not, they have work of their own to do. But if you frequently remind them of all the great things you do each day, come review time, they will also remember those things. As with all advice, you don't have to listen to this. Just know that if you aren't reminding your boss how great you are, I bet the person sitting in the cubicle next to yours is.

Not only should you be promoting yourself to your manager, but you should also self-promote to other managers in the company. In some companies, when it comes to reviews, promotions, and raises, there is a limited amount of money allocated to go around. The organization is told, you have X amount to spend on raises in total. Other companies might have a system that says the average percentage increase must be Y. This means that some people will get over that amount and others will get under, in order to keep the average. The management team will usually get together in a room and decide who gets what amount. In that meeting, you need your manager in the room making a case for you. To help them, it is favorable to have another manager agree with your manager, "oh yes, Bob is great." They might even tell a story about something Bob (aka you) did that impressed them. As more people are repeating the things you tell them of how great you are, the more likely you are to be on the high side of the curve instead of the lower side.

Managing your manager requires you to educate your manager in the way you want them to perceive you. Do you want them to see you as someone who sits at his or her desk all day and grumbles about not getting the recognition you deserve, or are you someone who wants to be perceived as the best most productive person on the team? If so, tell your manager how productive you are and all the great work you do.

Have you worked with someone who one day got promoted or moved into another role that you wanted? I bet you have. Then did you think to yourself, "What the fuck is the boss thinking? That person is useless!" What is it that person did to get themselves noticed? The self-promoter gets out and talks about what they do is they network and they tell everyone how great they are while trying to sound humble about it. The person who is skilled in self-promotion is the extrovert who comes across as valuable to the company without trying to be perceived as an attention whore.

There is an art to self-promotion, because there is a not-so fine line between self-promotion and being a braggart. How do you self-promote without coming across as bragging? Use this example as a template for how to have that conversation.

"How's it been going?" my manager asked.

"Busy week," I responded, "I was working on XYZ projects but I also spent a bizarrely large amount of time helping everyone else on the team out with their stuff."

"Oh, on what?" my manager asked.

"Mostly just answering questions on how to do things."

"Do you need anything from me to help clear up your schedule?"

"No, I'm good. I don't mind helping out so much; it's one of the prices I pay for being the one who knows the most about ABC."

In the above scenario, I gave my manager updates on the projects I was working on, while also calling out how I was going above and beyond my assigned work, by helping others out with their job, and showing my extra value to the company. Would my manager have known I was doing that without me telling him? Maybe. It is possible he would have seen it through casual conversation. It is possible someone I helped out would have mentioned it. But it is also possible that neither of those things would have happened, and if I didn't say something my manager wouldn't have known, and he would not have been aware of how great of an employee I was, by being so helpful to everyone else.

Self-promotion isn't just about you promoting yourself. The best method of self-promotion is to get others to do it on your behalf. So, let's say in the above example I mentioned how I was going out of my way to help others, and at the same time one of my peers mentioned this to my manager as well. We hear all the time about networking, network this, network that, network with those people, network yourself, social network, and it goes on. Networking is the way we promote ourselves in the modern world. We can network by posting articles on LinkedIn that the hundreds of people who follow us see. They then reference that article when talking to someone else, and our name gets out there.

In an office, the network we create involves other people doing some of the work for us. In the case of the above example, they can say, "It was great how Milo took time out of his day today to answer those questions. After answering the question, he wrote an article for our internal knowledge base so that everyone else can learn about the answer too." Look how great all that made me look. One, I received credit for answering the question. Two, I received credit for writing the knowledgebase article. And three, I get to avoid having to deal with someone coming and asking me the same question at a later date. Doing that work made me look good, while also enabling me to do less work later on.

I hosted a screening for an independent feature film once, and after the screening for this little indie film we did a QA with the creators of the film. We talked about the making, they told funny stories, we gave the audience the chance to ask some questions. Then at the end I was wrapping it up and an audience member shouted out this question, "Who are you?"

"Oh, did I not introduce myself?" I responded. "I'm Milo Denison, the show is called 'No Budget'..." etc.

This lead to one of the members of the crew saying, "We really want to thank the guys for putting this together." Along with a few other kind words in recognition of what we did for them. I didn't ask anyone to say that, nor did anyone ask the audience member to ask the question. In my opinion, the event was about the film, and giving the filmmakers an opportunity to promote their work. Yet at the end of the screening, by creating a fun positive environment for them, they showed the same kindness in return for me and my show. If I had started the interview talking about myself and the show, how great it was, and that everyone should watch it, I would have come across as someone who was more concerned about promoting himself. But by spending that time promoting others, they showed the same in return without the need for me to ask for it. It was not intentional, but we managed to get someone to positively promote me and my show.

In the YouTube series, there is often a copy of my book, An Expat's Guide to Ireland, in the background somewhere. It is a bit of shameless self-promotion on my part, but I don't actually bring the subject of the book up on the show. I simply set it in the background somewhere. Yet, occasionally one of my fellow cast mates will talk about the book, or a guest will reference it. I'm not actively promoting the book, at all but by simply having it sitting around, others are doing so on my behalf. Has this translated to an increase in sales? Based on the numbers the answer is no, but any word is a good word—or so they say. Want to translate this to the office? If you are receiving a cheesy award for something, be sure to have it on your desk somewhere. Take a few minutes (on the clock) to update LinkedIn with the awards received, so that others can see it when looking you up.

Perform the subtle work of self-promotion throughout the year, then review time will roll around, and when you are sitting in the manager's office, be sure to make everything you did sound like it was a great benefit to the company and the team. Did you answer some random question asked by someone? Make it sound like you are going above and beyond in helping that person, and had to go out of your way to do so. Did you have coffee with a friend of yours in another department? That isn't just coffee, that is cross-team alignment. Did you speak up during that meeting and volunteer to take on some extra work that you have no intention doing? As far as your manager knows, you plan to do it. And if not, it's your own great management skills that allowed you to delegate that work to someone else, you didn't pass the work off, you helped them to be more successful.

Managers and executives come and go all the time. When this happens, and your boss moves to another role, they will often sit down with the incoming manager and discuss each person on the team. When they get to you, they can either say, "Yep Bob is here and does stuff." Or they can describe you to the new manager as the person who gets things done and who is a productive go-getter. Even if you are not that person, they will up-sell you to the new manager, because you have done a great job of letting them know how valuable you are. Then when the new manager meets with you, they will already have an idea of how valuable to the team you are. You can then reinforce your value in your first meeting with them, in which you tell them all the great things you do. Just like that first interview, where you told the old manager of your greatness.

They say it's all about how you present yourself. If you present yourself as an indispensable asset to the company, people will begin to think you are indispensable. But don't let that go to your head. We are all dispensable, and everyone can be replaced—especially you.

Become an Extrovert

Think about the CEOs at most of the top companies in the world. One of the ways they contribute to the success of the company is by getting out from behind the desk and behaving in an extroverted way. They are in positions of authority because they have made it known that they deserve that authority. Their role is to make everyone aware of how extraordinary the company they lead is.

Anyone who worked for Microsoft during the Steve Ballmer years will recall him up on stage waving his arms, yelling, and sweating his way through his speeches. There can be no doubt that Steve is an inspiring extrovert, even though it could be argued that the other well-known Microsoft founder Bill Gates is more of an introvert. Richard Branson of Virgin is a very outgoing person, we often see him on television doing speeches, promoting his endeavors and living the lifestyle that many of us dream of living. Even though he has stated in his book *Losing my Virginity*[v] that he still gets nervous when doing interviews, he lives an extroverted person's lifestyle. Do you think most successful politicians are introverts or extroverts? I think we can agree that they are not the quiet, intellectual, reflective types, because if they were, we probably wouldn't know anything about them, and we probably wouldn't be giving them our vote. Politicians are required to get out on stage and impress on us the value they have to offer as our elected officials. Extroverts are charismatic, and feel comfortable getting up in front of people; they like the attention. Extroverts are considered as people who can motivate others. Extroverts are the ones that get attention in team meetings, in manager reviews, and by peers. Extroverts are the ones we often see being successful in a corporate environment. They might not be the best, but they do get success and recognition in return for their personalities.

I spent eight years working for AT&T, and during that time I had some good managers and directors, and other times, some not-so-good ones. At one point, I reported to a director called Karl, who was the epitome of an extrovert. During our team meetings, he would bounce around, he would get everyone in that room jazzed up. He would talk about the next great thing we were going to be working on, and we would leave the room with everyone onboard with whatever it was he wanted us to do that week. And that was the frustrating part, because what he wanted our focus to be on changed on a regular basis. "Milo, I want you to drop A and focus all your attention on B." "Ok," I would respond, with the same level of enthusiasm, and suddenly be all over whatever it was. The following week or two he would email me or call my desk asking, "Hey Milo, what's the status of A." "Um, I haven't done anything with it because you told me to work on B." "Ok, well now drop B and focus on A." It was frustrating to work for someone who seemed to have A.D.D. but for a while I was super enthused about whatever A or B was. The reason I bought into the enthusiasm at first was the same reason that everyone else did, because he was charismatic. Karl had a passion for the company and our products, that made us passionate as well. My enthusiasm waned as the frustration of the ever-changing priorities got to me. Eventually that director lost his enthusiasm for the company, and left for the next big thing, because as the exuberant extrovert he was, he needed that next big thing to keep him interested.

I´m sure we have all worked for someone who throws things out there, doesn't check in often, and then is surprised by the outcome. I'm not saying all extroverts are like that, but I am saying be aware of the extroverted, yet-also-can't-focus personality that sometimes goes along with it.

There was another flaw in the way Karl lead the organization, and that was in his focus on the *quick wins* and *low hanging fruit*. As a manager, it is important to look at the long-term strategy of an organization. But for him, it had more to do with looking good in the immediate short-term, receiving reward for those successes, while leaving everything else up in the air. We see this now on a national level, where politicians are focused only on the next election and winning that. They know that the voting populace doesn't care about long term results, only about what has happened in the short-term. So instead of looking to long term solutions for climate change, the national debt, and income inequality, they look for that quick win of passing a short-term spending bill, that reduces taxes for someone at the expense of the long-term problems facing the country. This is partially their fault for having a short-term focus, but the fault also lies with those who go along with it.

When it comes to behaving like an extrovert, be aware that working for an extrovert might not be the best time to behave like one. Often when someone likes to be the center of attention, they might not like it when someone else comes along and takes a bit of that attention away from them. We will get into this in the chapters on good and bad management types. If they are a good manager, even as an extrovert, they will let your star shine as much as their own. However, if they are not a good manager, it might be worth showing your extroverted side a little less when they are around.

There are, of course, exceptions to the rule that you need to be an extrovert in order to be successful. Everyone knows someone who is quiet and reserved, and who has moved ahead in the company. But in those cases, we need to take into consideration how good that person is at the job. I would argue an introvert has to be twice as good at the job to receive recognition in comparison to a standard extrovert. We need to think about how long they have been with the company, and how many people have seen them being brilliant in their work. The quiet person can come in and do great work every day, but it also might take a bit longer for the managers to become aware of it. Another example I will use is Dave, who had been working for the company for years before I arrived. He would quietly come in each day and do a job that far exceeded the role requirements. I don't know what he got on his reviews, but I imagine they were good, assuming his manager recognized how good he was. Because, if it came down to Dave telling others how great he was, no one would know.

Each month we would do an award for someone who went above and beyond. I was on the committee that reviewed the nominations each month, and month after month we would always see at least one nomination for Dave. But in the process, we might see a couple nominations for someone else, and depending on who wrote the nomination and how well it was written, Dave would usually get passed over for this monthly recognition. After a few months of this, we saw another nomination come in for him, and at that point we agreed that he was getting it regardless of the other submissions. At the team meeting where we called out Dave, I mentioned that he was quiet, not one to up-sell himself, and that the award had been long deserved. A few years later he eventually began to quietly move his way up the pyramid. But imagine that Dave were an extrovert.

Imagine him going into team meetings, getting up in front of everyone and talking about the great projects and initiatives he was doing. Imaging that he spent his time pointing out in presentations how much money he was saving the company, and the value he added. Imagine how quickly he would move up the ladder then. Dave is rare case, because he had a good management staff that could see the value he added, and they eventually recognized him for it. But what if he had had a bad manager? What if that manager hadn't seen how good he was? In that case, often the brilliant introvert will become frustrated in the corporate environment, and could either become disgruntled, eventually letting the quality of their work fall, or they might leave the company and move on to another one, only to repeat the cycle. This happens more often than companies would like to admit, especially in the larger corporations, where it is easy for people to be overlooked. The people who are often overlooked are the introverts, who don't self-promote as well as the extroverts do.

    Let's look at Bill Gates again, since you might be thinking that he is a well-known introvert who is one of the richest men in the world. Even Mr. Gates has to be an extrovert at times to get his points across. Another advantage Gates had, is that he was one of the founders of the company. He had the luxury of starting at the top, and the luxury of being a brilliant person who could see the future of technology. He also was good at something else:

gathering the right people around him. He was able to be the brains in a lot of ways, while letting others run the operations of the growing company. And it worked. Microsoft is now a massive company with over 100,000 full time employees. Mr. Gates is now using his genius at his foundation, trying to help the world as best he can. When watching him speak on the issues that his foundation is focused on resolving, he is soft spoken and intelligent, yet on occasion he might release a swarm of mosquitoes on a crowd as well, in order to get his point across. Warren Buffett, a friend of Bill Gates, and also very successful person, was so afraid of public speaking when he started out, that he took the Dale Carnegie course on public speaking.[vi] Warren Buffett is another who is forced to display a bit more of an extroverted manner at times.

For a lot of people, being an extrovert is difficult, and they find it draining to be that type person each day. They find it exhausting trying to be someone they are not. But it can also be rewarding, especially when they get that nice raise, and know that their dedicated self-promotion work is paying off. You know what they say, no one looks unhappy on a jet-ski, and raises pay for that jet-ski. You have to be the extrovert that is recognized as a "go getter" even though what you say might be total nonsense. In her book *"Quiet"*, Susan Cain[vii] gives examples of famous extroverts and introverts. The extroverts are usually the politicians and natural public speakers, and the introverts tend to be the writers and artists who enjoy living in their heads. But just because someone isn't naturally an extrovert, doesn't mean they can't become one. That is what the phrase "fake it until you make it" means.

There are many ingredients of success in the world, and one of the most obvious has always been being an outgoing, well-spoken personality that stands out in a crowd. To be a successful introvert, the key is to master the ability to act like extroverts. I would say this is even more necessary in the modern world of new startups popping up all the time. Entrepreneurs need to become the extroverted spokesman, who stands out in a crowd dominated by social media and short attention-span news cycles.

Elon Musk tweets regularly, he is always doing interviews, and has no problem going after people who disparage his products in the press or in the courts. He also happens to be the CEO of great companies like Tesla and SpaceX, two companies competing in very different markets. I don't know if he is an introvert or an extrovert by nature, but it is his extroverted behavior that contributes to his success. He sets lavish goals that others wouldn't even dream of setting, yet somehow he seems to reach those goals. Even if the goals aren't met like car production numbers, the fact that the news is talking about them, is advertising that he doesn't need to pay for. It shows an extreme confidence in his product.

Remember the Tucker 48? You probably don't recall it unless you watched the 1988 movie on

Preston Tucker [viii] or are a car aficionado. The car was revolutionary at the time in a lot of ways, but when it came to competing against giants GM and Ford, the Tucker couldn't keep up. Maybe if they had Twitter and a 24-hour media at the time, the results might have turned out more in the favor of Preston Tucker. Maybe in today's world the Tucker would be an all-electric, self-driven, hover car that half the country would own.

Getting back to us regular people, and forgetting about the Tucker and Tesla for a bit, how can those of us who are opposed to behaving like an extrovert stand out? Start slowly. When you are in a meeting and someone else is presenting, ask a question or make a comment. This might seem like a simple thing, but simple steps are the best way to start. By speaking out in meetings you will become used to the sound of your voice in front of others. The larger the meeting the more you should do this. Does your company have a large employee get-together with the higher-ups? If so ask some question. This sounds like a simple thing to do, but for some introverts, having that large of an audience for your question might be nerve-wracking. Once you do it and get the answer, sit back down and realize that it wasn't that bad.

Next, if your company has a Toastmasters society, join it. Toastmasters meet regularly to help people develop the skills required to speak in front of others. They are a supportive group with a global reach that have helped the introverts of the world thrive in a world of extroverts, or, at least, they have helped people who get nervous speaking in public to get over some of those nerves. Warrant Buffet had a massive fear of public speaking when he was younger. Knowing that in order to be successful he would need to overcome that fear, he took workshops to help him get over it. Now, looking at him speaking in pubic, you wouldn't really know it, and he's one of the richest men in the world. Yes, it's his genius that got him there, but through that, and his ability to work with and speak to others, he was able to get the financial backing needed to get to the top of his field.

Finally, start faking it until you make it. We have all probably heard this term at some point, and the reason it is often repeated is because it works. When an opportunity to present to a smaller group comes up take that opportunity. Practice what you need to present so that you are comfortable with the content, show it to just one peer or loved one in advance if you need to. The loved one isn't going to tell you it sucks; they are going to be supportive, which is what you need. The peer will point out anything that you may be able to do better. Take that advice and use it. If you have a good manager, bounce the presentation off them.

When you get to that larger meeting, take a breath and make the presentation. Even if you stumble, once it's done you will realize it wasn't that bad. Then the next one will be better, and then continue to make them. The nerves will never go away completely, but over time you will learn to manage them better. Start speaking up during meetings, and get used to the sound of your own voice. At first, you will know that you are faking that enthusiasm, but after a while it will become more familiar to you and easier. To use an old analogy; it's like riding a bike. At first you wobble and fall down, you feel foolish, and over time you learn to ride it properly. The introverted nerves might never go away, but that is okay. It is learning to handle them that contribute to success.

Know the Books

There are many books available to the world about how to run a meeting, run a project, learn your personality traits, or be great leaders. When it comes to working in a corporate environment. The books tend to be purchased by someone who wants to run projects, learn personality traits, and be a great leader. When your boss or some other executive talks about some book that they just read, about psychological safety through the soft-skills communication traits of others, you should pretend you have also read that book, even if you haven't, and don't have any intention of doing so. The reason is because the executives get a little hard in their pants when they find out that someone else has read it.

Honestly, most of the corporate advice and success books on the market are boring, trust me, I've read a lot of them over the years—usually at the recommendation of a peer or executive who felt the need to provide me with a copy. During my introduction to Microsoft, the director of my organization handed me a copy of something that he was kind enough to autograph, as if he had written it himself—he hadn't. That book sat at my desk for years after it was given to me. It might have been a good read with useful information, but on the list of things to read it never made it high enough on my list, primarily because I felt it was a bit pretentious of him to write in it and sign it. I eventually loaned it out to someone before I had a chance to read it, and it was never returned. No loss to me as far as I am concerned. Nevertheless, simply by letting it sit on my desk for years it made me look good. Similar to award certificates and other pro-corporate life paraphernalia that would sit on my desk, a bit of easy self-promotion.

What if you have a new Xbox or PlayStation at home, or maybe you have dinner plans with the cutie a few cubicles down? Or, let's simply say you have a life outside of the office, and are not interested in reading corporate speak self-help books? How can you look like a well-read employee who cares about your career, and is in touch with the latest fad in business management? Simple, you can just read the highlights on Amazon and bullshit your way through the conversation. One of the most important rules in managing your manager is bullshitting them into thinking you enjoy the same stuff they do. In fact, one of the most important rules in being successful at anything in the corporate world is the ability to effectively BS others. Speaking out of your butt and making it sound brilliant, in essence, is what this book is about. It doesn't matter if you haven't read that book on how horse riding relates to better business, because you think it was written by a pretentious know-it-all (like this one). All you really need to do is pretend you have read it, and thanks to the modern world, it is now much easier to do that.

> Example 1: *"Death by Meeting. A Leadership Fable"* by Patrick Lencioni.

The new manager asked if anyone had read it during his first team meeting with us. "Yes." I responded, having never even heard of the book prior to that day.

"What did you think?" He asked.

"I thought it was really interesting," I responded. "Most of it was common sense, like have an agenda, and keep meetings short." but it was still a worthwhile read.

Notice what I did? I mentioned something that was in the book, validating that I read it, and by commenting on what I thought of it, I was showing him that I have an opinion on the subject matter, and had given some thought to what is in the book. Technically, I have now read the book, and it has more to do with open discussions during meetings, and explains that conflict is good for productive discussions. This is advice I actually agree with, and feel that more companies would do well to follow it. Honestly, I don't recall at all if it has a chapter on having a meeting agenda, but what the book is actually about is beside the point, and doesn't really matter, because we can tell a lot of what it is about, based on the title. As intelligent people, we can deduce a couple of areas that the book probably spends at least a few pages discussing. Any book on running a meeting is going to suggest using an agenda, and even if it doesn't, meeting agendas are something that has been so ingrained into our psyche that I could make it sound like it was in the book. Not many people have a perfect memory when it comes to stuff they read, and so, even if the manager thought to himself that he didn't remember that part, he would also believe it was in there, because it makes sense that some section of the book would mention agendas. And by saying that it's mostly common sense, it implies that I already had a pretty good idea on how to run a meeting. It took me no effort, and I managed to look to the new boss like I cared about bettering myself in the business.

> Example 2: *"The One Minute Manager,"* by Ken Blanchard.

> "I like his emphasis on keeping conversations short and to the point."

I know nothing about this book besides the title. The title makes me think it has to do with managers not wasting a lot of time when interacting with people. It might not, but I'd be willing to say that if I was ever in a meeting of others who might have read it.

Do you have a phone on your pocket? Is there a laptop in front of you at most meetings? What can you do quickly with both of those items? You can hold your phone under the desk or table and do a quick search on a book someone mentioned and read the summary. You can open a browser window and look up that book on a laptop. By the time the person is done talking about the book, you could have read the description, giving you enough information to pretend to have read it.

A study in 2013 polled 2,000 people in Britain. Of the respondents, 62% said they would pretend to have read the book if they were discussing a book they had not read,[ix] If the Brits can do it so can you. Instead of office-related nonsense, can you honestly say you have never gone along with someone who was talking about *"The Catcher in the Rye"* as if you had read it. It's such a well-known book after all, that everyone should read it. You wouldn't want to deal with the speaker's indignant look at hearing you haven't, so you nod your head in agreement. Or perhaps *"Catch 22"* the one you have seen a few clips from the movie. Based on a few scenes from the movie it probably wouldn't be too hard to pretend to have read the book.

Personally, I like reading of almost any sort; I have often read books like *"The Purple Cow"* when they have recommended to me, and *"The Richest Man in Babylon."* After all, who doesn't want to be rich? If we can read a book on the subject, and it suddenly happened based on the advice given, we might as well do it. If you want to BS your way through *"The Richest Man in Babylon"* it's mostly about saving money. Save a little money each month, invest it if you can, and by the time you are dead you will be the richest man. That might be over simplifying the book a bit, but you can read it and decide for yourself what the lesson in the book is.

Being viewed well in the eyes of others, as a reader of these so-called self-help books isn't for everyone, I totally understand and accept that. The nice thing is, that many of the corporate self-help books are similar, so if you read one, you can probably BS your way through another. Even this book could be used to talk your way through others on the subject of managing managers and self-promotion. Managerial types or personality types are pretty common, so the section on that, in this book, probably isn't going to be all that different from an entire book on the subject. This book just summarizes it down to two chapters instead of a whole book. Now that you are reading this one, and will read it all the way through, since it is a fascinating read, when you are done you can go and play the latest *Assassins Creed* game or catch the latest superhero flick at the theatre. Then tomorrow, go along with a conversation that someone might be having on successful introverts.

I have written quite a bit in this chapter on the subject of faking or pretending we have read a few of the office related self-help books. But as an avid reader, it is important for this author to make the case for actually reading books, as it might contribute to a person's success. Or, if not contribute to success, then at least make a person smarter. Henry David Thoreau said, "A truly good book teaches me better than to read it. I must soon lay it down, and commence living on its hint. What I began by reading, I must finish by acting." When we read something of value we don't just get to say we have read something that makes us sound super smart, like that douchebag who brags about reading *"The Art of War."* Hopefully, we can get something out of a good or useful book that can be incorporated into our lives. A good example of this is the previously mentioned book, *"Quiet"* by Susan Cain. Often, introverts feel the need to hide their introverted natures. After all, the chapter on becoming an extrovert is on the subject of pretending to be something you are not. Yet in the book, Susan Cain makes a case for being an introvert, and provides useful advice for an introvert living in an extroverted world. As someone myself who prefers the silence of a forest over the hustle and bustle of the city, and has anxiety attacks at the thought of meeting new people or being in social environments, I was able to take a lot of the advice in the book to heart: advice about living in an extroverted world, but making sure I take time to myself, to allow my introverted tendencies to recover.

Since you are reading this book, it implies you are hoping to get something out of it that will make you more successful in your job. This is something I, too, hope you get out of it, or else the massive amount of time I spent in front of my computer writing, and the gallons of ingested coffee and tea, will all have been for nothing.

Dumb-it-Down

My initial presentation had 22 very detailed PowerPoint slides. I had spent weeks working on it, reviewing it, and making sure all my graphs were in order and the math was correct. A proper summary was included to start the presentation off. Following the summary was a slideshow of the scenarios that our customers were finding themselves in, including a lot of smart objects to make it easy and entertaining to follow. From there I had a proposed solution, the customer impact that we would see from the solution, including metrics and everything anyone could possibly need to make the correct decision. The correct decision, as far as I was concerned, was to move forward with the project. Technically the initial project wasn't even my idea. The project was brought to me by a manager on another team who had proposed it, but didn't have the bandwidth to move forward with it. She brought me into work on it with her, as I had time to manage the project to fruition. The proposal had been discussed with a few people prior to the meeting; I already had buy-in from my local management team, so I went into the meeting relatively confident that the project would be approved and would move forward.

The project seemed like an easy win for me. The customers would benefit, the company would look good, and most importantly I would come across as a skilled project manager. Especially since, at the time, I was looking to move into a full-time project management role. I saw this as a good opportunity to add to my resume of successes and increase my standing in the company.

The purpose of the presentation and conference call I was on, was to get the approval needed to move to the testing stage. This purpose of the presentation was to take it to other higher-ups for approval to move it forward. The higher-ups were the director of my organization, and the managers who reported to her. The medium I was using for the presentation, however, was a conference call with the director (The HIPPO), in a room full of managers, at a remote location. As anyone who has been on remote conference call knows, it can be difficult to keep the attention of others. Often, people will sit and go through emails, work on something else, or just mentally space off when being presented with things over the phone via a Skype meeting. I know I do. In fact, I would often use remote conference calls as an opportunity to clear out my email inbox, so I couldn't fault others for doing the same.

By the time, I was done with the presentation, there were multiple questions. Having done my due diligence, I thought I was prepared for any questions that might arise. You could view that as a good thing that they asked questions, leading me to assume that they had been paying attention. However, some of the questions had already been clearly answered in the presentation, and others were completely unrelated. One manager was more concerned by what our engineering team would think, versus our customers—who were the ones we were supposed to be focused on. One aspect of this project involved being more forthcoming with customers about development errors and fixes that were in the works. Another manager wanted to know the impact of the teams' workload. A valid question, as it would have an impact—except that I had already gone over the impact on the workload in the presentation, and if he had been paying attention he would have known the answer. By the end of the meeting, I didn't have the approval that I wanted; instead I had a bunch of action items.

I could have ended it there, moved the project to an incomplete status and moved on to the next initiative. It would have been easy to do, as there was plenty of other things to work on. But I wasn't quite ready to give up on it yet, and I knew that if we could make this happen it would be a success for the team and the company. Or at least it would be a success for me in a role that I was trying to establish myself in, because in reality, I knew this project required a little too much internal coordination and communication. These were both skills that I didn't see as something the organization was all that good at. There was too much manual work involved in this, and as a project coming from someone at my level, I could tell that it would be something that would happen, last for a few months, then slowly fizzle out.

Instead of getting disgruntled about the lack of approval I was looking for at the time, I went back to my initial presentation and thought to myself, how can I make it short, simple, and easy for people to follow without the need for me to explain it? One of the issues, in my opinion, was that the project presentation wasn't clear and to the point. It was long and overly detailed. Yes, I had every bit of information anyone could need on the proposal, but when it came to someone sitting on another continent being presented with something they didn't come up with, it had to catch their attention.

My first stop was the manager sponsor of the project to solicit her feedback, and to learn what could be cut and revised in the presentation. Based on that feedback I took it to one more person for additional feedback. We are often afraid to solicit feedback from others, as it is deemed negatively in our own minds as if we have failed in some way. Depending on the feedback, however, often the person you are talking to might take it as a good thing. Approaching your manager to ask, "how can I make this better or improve this?" makes you come across as someone who is willing to solicit feedback and take it to heart. This is one of those skill sets that managers look for in good employees, and it is what I did in this situation. They love to see someone take that feedback and act upon it. It makes them feel good, as, the resource that you call on, and makes them feel useful, because they had the answers. This is also something to look for in a manager. They need to be able to provide good feedback, and to support you, making you a better employee and therefore making them a better manager.

Taking the feedback I had received, I began reducing the presentation down, eventually ending up with three slides. The presentation still included enough graphics to make it visually interesting but limiting it to include only the basic pieces of information. I also worked through the list of actions items I had been previously requested to answer. The new three-page PowerPoint had almost no detailed information and simply a problem, a proposed solution, and benefit to the company. This is really all that they needed to see at that point, this was the dumbed-down version after all. If anyone had questions or wanted to know more, they could reference the long presentation, but when it comes to decision making, most decisions are made based on an initial gut instinct. Look at the modern political system and voters, for example. A person isn't necessarily elected on their knowledge of the issues and intelligence; they are often elected due to the emotional reactions of the voters. Office politics and project approvals work in a similar manner. We want to present just enough information to get the recipient excited, but not so much as to get bogged down in the details. Yes, have the answers ready for those who want to know the details, but don't start off with them.

The second time I dialed into the Skype call with the same group of people, I walked them through the reduced slideshow. I was asked a couple of questions, none of which were related to the previous action item list that had since been forgotten, and which I had no intention of bringing up if no one else did. Thirty minutes later the project received it is approval. Nothing had really changed in terms of the content, I wasn't more prepared in any way, all I did was dumb it down, focusing on just the key pieces of information. I still had the larger 22-page presentation for anyone who wanted to review it, and I included both presentations in the meeting notes that were sent out later. Presentations and project approvals are not about making yourself look like the smartest person in the room, although some think it is. Project presentations are about knowing your audience and in some situations, and that could mean creating multiple versions of the same presentation for each audience. Approvals are about getting the approver excited about the project; very few people are excited about detailed lists and metrics. Just be sure to have that information to hand for the few people who are excited about it and want it.

The lesson here is to know your audience, then to present the information as simply as possible, while avoiding it looking like a simplified version. The higher up you move within a company, the less you know. This isn't meant as an insult, it is the truth, in the sense that we all know what we need to know. Someone who has multiple things on their mind, who is thinking of the next meeting they need to attend, or who is going through and replying to emails at the same time, couldn't really care less about your detailed presentation. So why go through the effort to make it overly complicated for someone who really doesn't care? Make it simple and pretty to look at, and get that approval, then move on. The benefit for you is, the simpler you make it, the less work you need to do. Don't expect that senior manager to know the details of the code you had to write, or the way you tweaked that Excel chart to make it display the information in the best way. Expect that senior manager to know very little about what you do in a given day, and don't look at that as an insult. Look at it as an opportunity to show them what you want them to see, and get the approval you want from them, so that you can continue with your work (surfing Facebook), and they can go back to doing whatever it is they do that earns them the high pay they receive.

The reason you were hired by the company is to be an expert in the job you are doing, so don't expect the person you are working for to be an expert in it too. Think of every presentation or meeting as the first day of school and you are the teacher. The teacher doesn't walk into class and start teaching advanced algebraic equations. The teacher goes in and dumbs it down for the students, eventually building them up throughout the course to be experts. The difference between a teacher and you, for your presentation, is that it is always the first day of class, and you are the teacher.

Get Others on Your Side

If you don't promote yourself, who will? In the section on self-promotion, we talked about promoting yourself to your manager, and to those around your manager. Yet there is something even better than you talking yourself up, and that is getting others to do it on your behalf. Sometimes, when speaking highly of oneself we can come across as a blowhard. This is a curse most Americans suffer from. We think that, by constantly talking about how great we are, it reinforces that information in others. In reality, it just makes us look like a bunch of arrogant assholes. In essence the largest economy, with the largest military, and biggest companies, can't have people taking about the greatness of it all. We have to be humble. Working in the corporate office is the same, just on a smaller scale. By getting others to talk about how great we, are it comes across a lot better than invading someone's office and informing them how amazing we are.

When hearing this it sounds pretty nice. "Oh, Joe said I was super helpful on setting up that clients account? That's very nice of him, but really I was just being supportive. Not a big deal." When we hear of a person being spoken highly of by someone else, it comes across as more genuine and believable. "Did you see that pivot table Frank included in the presentation for the client? Man, that guy sure knows his way around a chart." Compared to, "Did you see my pivot table in that chart? It was fantastic wasn't it? One of the greatest." Or, "Joe didn't tell you all the work I did helping him out. Well, I did a lot of work on it. If it weren't for me we wouldn't have made that sale."

Now, if you don't promote yourself, who will? The people you get to do it for you; that's who. In the self-promotion chapter, we had an example that involved me telling my manager how I was taking time out of my day to help others. It was true, I was frequently interrupted throughout the day, and spent a large amount of my time helping others in that particular role. But if the information had emanated from me alone, it could have come across as if I was bothered or complaining, which could have been viewed as being negative. The better solution was to arrange it so that when my manager had a one-on-one meeting with one of my peers, he or she would also say something about me being helpful. The information I provided the manager about being helpful was then being reinforced by another person as well. One plus one equals looking like a champ.

Some of your peers are probably reading articles or books like this and following the advice on promoting themselves. That is why there are so many websites, news articles, and books on the subject of self-promotion, because people read them. People want to look like the star. Yet, not all of those books talk about getting others to talk about how great you are. They might cover the subject lightly, but usually it is about being confident, about documenting your successes, and having a positive attitude. Yes, do all that, but more importantly, spend a little time making friends with your co-workers. Spend some time getting the people who work with you to talk you up to others.

    The first and easiest way is bribery, and no, not the slip someone some cash type of bribery. Most large companies have awards programs that people can nominate others for. Remember that time a co-worker asked you for help on something? Be sure to remind them when it comes time to submit nominations for the awards programs. I once worked for a company where we had this kudos system. It was simply an internal website we could access, and give someone a kudos for helping out, or for going above and beyond. Eventually, if we got enough of them each quarter we would receive gift certificates. But more important than the certificates, was that during review time we could say how many we had received that quarter. This was often where I would shine at that company, because I would usually receive more than most of the rest of the team. We also had levels of awards, and I would usually be in the top five to reach the higher levels. Some of my peers reached that level due to working hard and helping others without asking for a kudos in return. I reached it through hard work (most of the time) and helping others while also asking for a kudos in return. I did the same work as others, I would just remind my peers as I helped them to show a little recognition.

Those of us that were at this top tier were there for two reasons. The first and obvious reason is we did help people out and took up a large portion of each day solving problems for others. The second reason was that whenever someone said "Thanks for the help," after providing them with help, people like me would then often respond with, "Nothing says thanks like a kudos." They knew what I meant by this and usually later at some point that notification would arrive in my email box, with my manager copied in it, containing the details of what I had done that was so helpful.

At a previous company, they had something similar, where we could nominate people with a write-up. Then a select group of people would review those write-ups and reward a handful of employees with a trip—usually to Hawaii. I was never on that trip, but I knew a few people who were. Those people did a good job, but not necessarily much better than I did. Nor did they necessarily do better jobs than others whom I knew were better performers than me. What they did better, however, was promote themselves, and get others to promote them as well.

One way of getting others to promote you is at review time. During annual reviews, many corporations have a system of soliciting feedback from peers. One company I worked for had an electronic system. I would put in the name of the person I wanted feedback from, and it would send an email to that person requesting feedback, and they could do the same to me. I never sent it to someone of whom I wasn't confident would provide positive feedback. Often, this would involve a conversation in advance consisting of, "I'll give you good feedback and you give me good feedback." It was a win-win for both of us, especially if we reported to separate managers and the raises came out of different budgets.

A former co-worker of mine learned this the hard way. He solicited feedback from people he worked with regularly as instructed by his manager. One of the people he sent a feedback request to wasn't the greatest person and gave negative feedback. The thing is, Allen was by far a better performer than me at the job. He worked harder than I did, had a better attitude, and actually cared about the job. But since he solicited feedback from the wrong person, the management team was able to use that one negative review to lower his overall performance score and the amount of raise he received; while I received a better performance review and raise that year. Allen eventually left the job and went on to bigger and better things with another company. Do you think he made that mistake at the next company? I doubt it. He worked just as hard, and cared just as much, the lesson he learned was who to get on his side in advance of reviews. He is now doing very well for himself at the new company.

Let's move on from financial rewards and promotions and look at projects. Even if you are not a project manager by title or trade, it is very likely that you will be given projects to work on. The success of the project can be a form of recognition for reviews and promotions. So how, then, do we make our projects a success?

When we have social conversations, this can be a great opportunity to get others to go along with a proposal prior to any official meetings or presentations. The nice thing about doing this is that it gives us an opportunity to get the person we are talking to onboard with our idea. As people, we are often predisposed to being polite during face-to-face conversations. It is the same philosophy that sales people use; they prefer in-person conversations when trying to secure a sale. By talking face-to-face we have a captive audience, and the listener is less likely to want to make the speaker feel bad, by saying that the idea sucks. In the corporate world, once we have received some type of verbal commitment from the person, they are more likely help us out at a later point. Then, when it comes to the big presentation, they can also speak on our behalf as we have already got them onboard.

I was working on an initiative which involved a process change for a global team. The project was a simple support process change. The change, depending on how you looked at it, could create more work or reduce it. But we wouldn't know for sure until we launched the pilot. The pilot was a smaller project that tested the feasibility of the idea, and allowed us to work out the kinks before a full rollout. The catch was, that even to do the pilot, we needed multiple people on a leadership team to sign-off on it. Making it even harder was the fact that the signoff involved people who worked remotely, some of whom I had never even met face-to-face. In my mind the initiative made perfect sense, it was changing the organizational structure from a reactive one to a proactive one, it would increase customer satisfaction, and from the data, I believed it would probably reduce calls to the company's support organization. But when it comes to working with some engineering teams, the customer isn't as much of a focus as they say it is. Have you ever used something such as an app, or piece of software and thought, "who the hell designed this?" That would be an engineer with little real-world experience.

With this particular project, my first conversation was with my manager to make a case for it. This gave her the opportunity to throw out suggestions, and by incorporating her ideas I was quickly able to get her onboard. The next step was to find someone else who was working on a similar project, so that I could consolidate both projects into one. Since this other person had already received some approvals, they were combined with mine. After that, we added another person to the project, getting more people onboard, who would spread the word about the great thing we were working on. At that point there had been no official project kickoff meeting, all we had were some ideas and some side conversations. After identifying the core project team, I began looking at metrics, and putting together the formal presentation, all while continuing to have side office conversations. "What do you think of this?" I'd ask some managers and decision makers. They would respond with, "sounds like a good idea." The other people already working on the project were doing the same, and my manager helped to get her manager's buy-in as well. As we began to socialize it, we signed more people up for the idea. But when it came to the big day, presenting it to the leadership team, there was another manager who only liked ideas if they were his own ideas. And there was the decision maker, who happened to be located remotely. When it came to decision time, she wasn't quite onboard yet, even though we had all our ducks in a row. But she also wasn't saying "no". In a large organization like this one, this is how we make progress.

By that point, the seed was planted, and we could continue to work the proposal. The manager who was the one who only liked his own ideas, and was often not interested in listening to others was the hard yes for the project. Since I was at a junior level, the key wasn't in convincing him myself, but to have already had enough conversations with his peers, for those other managers to take the argument to him on my behalf, without my involvement at all. Once that was done the rest was easy. The decision maker was the kind of person who would listen to those who reported to her, and take their feedback into her decision making process. In the end, the decision was made, one to me that seemed obvious, and which, in a small organization, would have only taken a few weeks to implement, yet in this large one it took months. But in the end, it was done, and I could check that off as a success to my manager, who then checked it off as a success to her manager, so we both looked good. And when it comes to managing your manager, making them look good makes you look good.

There was once an executive whose name I don't recall, he left a large fortune 500 company, and one of the reasons he gave for leaving and going to a startup, was that the large corporation was like steering a cruise ship. It will turn but it will do it very slowly.

When it comes to getting others on your side, be sure to get the right people on your side and not the wrong ones. This should include assistants and admins. You would be surprised in a corporate environment how much sway the bosses' admin has with what happens in the office. In addition, sometimes, when making friends with co-workers, you can befriend the wrong people, and when they go down, through that association you get dragged down with them.

A tip for making friends in a corporate environment is to give credit to others. This can benefit you in multiple ways. One of which is that we get what we give. If you are talking about how great your peer is to someone, and that peer hears about it, they are more inclined to do the same for you. Another bonus is that you look like the positive person that you want to be perceived as. So that way, when someone potentially has an issue with you at a later date, the person they are talking to about you might not believe them, because you are such a great guy or girl.

Use the Slang

During my time at one specific company, each year we would have some new phrase that everyone seemed to be using. As far as I know, it was not because the executives or management teams got together and decided what the word or phrase was going to be. It just seemed to happen. My guess is someone took some workshop or read something that would get the word started in the daily lingo. For example, one year it was *Synergies* before moving to *Customer Centricity* the following year. It doesn't really matter what the phrase is, just find out what it is and use it. Throw synergies or whatever your company is using that month into as many presentations as possible. *Be bold* but don't over-use it, try to limit it to about three references per presentation. You want *engagement* with your slide-deck. I know it might come across as over-used and annoying, but believe me, your manager will love it, keeping in mind that our audience for any of this is our manager or their manager. The presentation is not made for who we actually think it is for, such as the client, partner team, or peers. I used to make it a bit of a game to use each of the annual phrases in the same presentation. Such as, "By implementing this process change we should be able to boldly engage our partner synergies through customer centric service solutions." No one ever noticed that I was doing it, or if they did, they didn't say anything. And by having fun with the phrase-of-the-year it makes things like creating boring presentations and delivering them a bit more fun.

Action Items
"The action items taken in notes from the last meeting are…"

Bandwidth
This one drove me nuts. Why can't people just say time? "I don't know if I have the bandwidth, let me do a quick speed test on my computer and see what the bandwidth is it is running at."

Deliverable
"Can you get me that deliverable by the end of the week?"

Due Diligence
I had a director once who used this all the time, as if he needed to continue to repeat it in order to simply get us to do our jobs properly.

Drill Down
"Can we drill down into that?" You mean look at it in more detail? Or do you mean get out a drill and make a hole in it?

Going Forward or Moving Forward
"Going forward we would appreciate it if you muted yourself on conference calls so people wouldn't hear you make fun of them."

HIPPO (highest paid person's opinion)
Don't actually use this acronym but always be aware of who that is.

Impact
"The impact on the audience will be a 10% increase in for the next fiscal quarter."

Low Hanging Fruit
Remember Karl from the chapter on being an extrovert? He loved this term. I wanted to take some of that fruit and throw it at him. Yes, let's pick the easiest thing possible to do this and do that, why bother with the hard stuff.

Proactive
Oh, they love this. When a person is proactive they are the one who moves ahead, so be sure to refer to yourself as proactive as often as possible. "I'm so proactive that I already started that presentation knowing it would need to be done."

Ping

When messaging on whatever messaging app you use as work, say "ping" instead of instant message. "Hey, can you ping me when you have a moment." And when asked, of course you have "bandwidth" to look at that.

RTRT (Release to Real Tester)

This is one myself and a friend used while working software releases. The development teams would generally check their own work and usually not do the best job. They would then release the product to the customers. Then when we would start getting calls with problems which they would fix based on customer complaints. The real tester being the customer. Think about this one next time you upgrade right away to a new program or app and it doesn't work.

Take it Offline

This is another one that drives me nuts. Can't people just say, "let us talk about it later when there is not a bunch of people sitting around a conference table to hear us?" Okay maybe that's saying a lot. Take it offline it is.

Touch Base

"Let's touch base and discuss this later."

I'm going to end with just these, as there are hundreds if not thousands of them. These were just the ones often used in locations I worked in, and still have traumatic memories about. Except for RTRT, because that one is just funny to realize the mindset of some in a corporate environment.

Yes, and...

This is something that is taught to improvisational theatre students. When on stage with other improv actors, one actor will say or do something, and the other actor is taught not to block what the first actor did. For example, an actor says, "We met on a train to Amsterdam full of sock puppets" The second actor wouldn't respond with "no we didn't." That would kill the scene because there wouldn't be anywhere to go from there. The audience would think that the skit wasn't very interesting, and it would throw the whole pace off. In improvisation, it is better to respond with a "yes," then add to what the previous person said or did. For example, "Yes, we did, and it was on that sock puppet train that we made sweet, sweet love for the first time." See how that works better than responding with a, "No we didn't"? The scene moves on with a "Yes and..." potentially leading to more humor, as each actor plays back and forth to see how far the scene goes before ending it. They can take the scene to anywhere they want, making sock puppet jokes, or whatever else comes to mind, if a person were to make love on a train full of sock puppets.

What does this have to do with managing your manager? Imagine if your manager comes up to your desk, and asks you to look at the numbers on the

TPS reports that have been sent out that month. Instead of responding with, "Why?" or "The TPS reports are pointless," or "People don't read those," you can respond with "Yes, and would you also like me to send those metrics to the rest of the management team?" Not only do you look good for agreeing to do it, you also look good for taking the initiative and offering to send it to others. Those other managers might read it and think of the great work you do. You would have had to get the metrics together anyway, even if you had started with a "why" instead of a "yes." So, you might as well look good when doing the work, and get as many bonus points for doing the work as possible.

Remember that time your boss asked you to stay late because some deadline needed to be met? And your instant thought was to tell him no, because a new episode of your favorite reality show was on that night? Instead of telling him the truth, you reluctantly agreed to do what he asked. The manager probably didn't think much of it because you didn't make it seem like a big deal. Instead of reluctantly agreeing, try "yes and…"

"Yes, I can stay late tonight and get that done. And if you like, I could also update the presentation slide with that data as well. It might take me a bit longer and I'll have to cancel dinner plans with my wife but at least that way it will be ready to go for tomorrow."

"Yes and…" then make the requester understand that you were going out of your way to help them out, potentially getting your wife mad at you, when in reality all you wanted to do was watch a crappy TV show that you could record or download the next day. The manager will feel a bit guilty about making you work late; he will credit you for it later and might ask the person at the desk next to yours next time, knowing the value you place on your family. You can take the credit now with a "yes" and set yourself up for the reward later.

Where does "yes and" get you? It gets you in the mind of managers as the go-to person; the one who is motivated, the one who gets stuff done. Even if you are not that person and you could care less about being the motivated go-to person. Pretending you are a motivated go-getter is good enough, especially since it is all work you would have to do anyway. Yes, some people actually are motivated to do extra work, some people care about their jobs, and they want the shareholders of the company to make more money. Okay maybe they don't care about the shareholders, but it is likely that they want the company to do well, thinking that they will receive a small portion of that success. Most of us are not that person, most of us are the person who comes into the office and works because it gives us money to do the things we want to do, to live in the places we want to live, and to buy us the stuff we want to buy.

In his book *"Start with Why"* Simon Sinek[x] advises us that "Great companies don't hire skilled people and motivate them. People are either motivated or they are not." In the perfect world, this would be true, and I would agree with Simon. In a perfect world, we would all be motivated to love our jobs, to believe in the project we are working on, and the products we sell or the service we offer. Often, we are actually motivated at the time we are hired, but as time wears on, I would argue that many people lose that motivation.

Over time, as a company grows, it needs people to fill seats. The people who get those seats might have a good resume that gets them into the interview. Or at least it is formatted with the correct keywords and exaggerated experience to get into the interview. But that person might not necessarily be the most motivated, or the right person for the job. And if you want it, that person could be you! All you have to do to come across as the motivated person who cares, is start sentences with a yes. Starting a sentence with a "yes" is a sign of motivation, and a sign that you care about whatever it is that was said before that.

As a manager, the job is to motivate people. Then when the manager sees that sense of caring in their subordinates, they feel a sense of accomplishment. They feel that they have made a difference, and had a positive impact on those who work for them. It gives managers that warm fuzzy feeling inside. As an employee, we need to make those managers believe that the warm fuzziness is true, because if we don't, when it comes to review time we will be the one who gets flagged as not caring, and as someone who isn't "onboard" with whatever it is we should be onboard with.

So how do we make our manager think we are the motivated one, the one that cares, the one who should get promoted, get the raise, and get the nice office with a window? Respond with the words "yes and…" when she asks you to do something. Then make it look like you are doing more while actually doing what you would have been doing in the first place.

To reference another book, Tim Ferris in the *"4-Hour Workweek"* [xi] writes, "Doing less meaningless work so that you can focus on things of greater personal importance is not laziness." The point he is making, is that by properly managing work and outsourcing if possible, we are then focusing our time on the important stuff. For me, at one point it was outsourcing gift vouchers for a photography studio. Initially, if someone ordered a voucher I would get an email, and then have to open up a template, update the template and email that to the client. It was a lot of manual work. It also involved me constantly monitoring my email inbox. So, instead, I outsourced. It cost a bit of money to have a service do it, but the time saved for me not having to constantly check emails and do manual work made up for it by freeing me up to do other things.

What does this have to do with "yes and..."? Nothing really, it is just a bit of good advice. Outsource if possible to free up time. And it makes me look well-read by referencing another book in this little book of mine.

Most of us don't have the option of outsourcing, so we spend most of our days doing work we don't care about at all. We do it because it's part of our job. We do it because we have to. If we can't outsource or de-prioritize some of this work, then we might as well make it look like we are going above and beyond by doing it.

When working on a contract assignment for a company at one point, my manager said something that was actually positive, but could have been taken as a negative. He said, "Milo does a really good job of knowing what he needs to know and no more." The reason I took this as a compliment instead of an insult, is that often it is easy to get drawn into work that doesn't affect us on a daily basis. When it came to the software I was working on, my role was coordinating the testing of it. My job consisted of working with project and program managers on test scenarios for the next upgrade. Then I worked with the testers to make sure they went through those scenarios, and submitted feedback to the development teams, in order to implement changes and fix bugs before the release. My job was not to be an expert on the product. Yes, I knew how it worked and I knew the basics that were needed to do the job, but I didn't know how engineers did their job, and I didn't know the ins and outs of the product. It wasn't necessary to know that for the job I did, that would have involved spending extra time and energy on stuff that wasn't relevant to me. I worked normal eight-hour days, unlike many of my peers, and yet I still managed to look like a success to that manager. I wasn't aware of it at the time, but the reason I was initially successful at the job, was that I responded with yes to each request he had made to me, and I responded by adding to his requests. But I still managed to do it while not doing unnecessary work that would have added to my workday.

A word of caution about "yes and...": when you do this and follow through with something, or go above and beyond, it can back backfire. If you do it too much, you can end up in a position where people start to take advantage of your good nature. At some point, you might get tired of doing this on every occasion and eventually say no. Then what happens? People might get mad at you for saying no, not realizing that you aren't saying no to regular work, you are saying it to the extra work. So, use "yes" with caution. This is also what happened to me in that testing role I mentioned earlier. I eventually started to push back, because I was no longer adding any value to the project. However, the nice thing about it being a contract assignment was, when everyone realized that I had done the work I was initially hired to do, and didn't want to do any of the extra work anymore, they ended the contract and I was able to move into another role.

How do we say no then? Often, I am asked by people to help them out with film or video projects. Usually they are produced by poor filmmakers looking to pay little or nothing at all. I do occasionally say yes, as this creates goodwill, and I can ask them for a favor at a later date. But saying yes too often, and your schedule will become overloaded. To resolve this, I put a limit on the number of people I will help out simultaneously at any given time. So, if someone comes to me and says, "Hey Milo can you help me out with this?" my response might be, "I would love to but I'm currently involved in projects x and y and just can't take on any more at this time. Your project sounds great and I am looking forward to seeing it when it is done." I will even ask them to send me a trailer or other link about it, and post it to my social network in order to help them promote the project.

The key to saying no is to do it in a way that doesn't burn that bridge. People know that others are busy, so letting the person know how busy I am justifying my saying no. It is also a good idea to provide them with a little positive reinforcement on the success of their project. Posting to social networks takes almost no time at all, and helps them a little.

In the corporate world, many of the chapters in this book have examples of showing others how much work you are doing. Self-promoting, becoming an extrovert, and getting others on your side, all involve showing your bosses and peers how much work you do for the company, and all the value you add. This is also a benefit in situations where you might need to say no to someone. "Sorry, I just don't have time to help out with that right now. I've got all these projects that I'm working on and deadlines I have to meet." Since I meet with my manager regularly, and let her know how busy I am, she won't question it when I have to say no to something.

Your time is precious, so when saying yes, be sure to get the credit for it, and look like the overachiever, but don't go too far with it, and if you need to say no to something, don't just say no, justify it. That way even with a no you are still developing a good relationship with that person, which could be beneficial at a later date.

Customer Service of Everything

Since we have a broad statement in our lexicon about the Internet and technology called the 'Internet of things', in which everything is connected to the Internet, we should also have something called the 'customer service of everything.' It is the same broad statement used to encompass just about every interaction we have with another person in life.

As part of the series *No Budget* I often get the opportunity to interview and talk to independent filmmakers. We had arranged to meet with an Irish filmmaker named Cashell to discuss a short film he made called *The Clockmaker's Dream*. The film was screening at a festival in a small coastal town south of Dublin called Dun Laoghaire. One of our producers had arranged to meet with him before the screening at the hotel showroom where his film was showing. We figured we could just find a quiet corner to set up the camera and use a hand-held mic for the quick interview. We had been to the hotel the previous year for the festival and done something similar.

The four of us arrived and looked around for a quiet space. The bar to the right didn't have anyone working behind the counter and the tables were empty, so we decided to set up to the side, next to a large window. Not wanting to stand out, we hadn't brought lighting with us, so the natural light came in handy. We also didn't check with the hotel or the festival in advance, which is also why we didn't bring a lot of gear with us, not wanting to take up a lot of space. This was all in an attempt not to get into anyone's way.

First things first, which involved heading back to the open bar area that was serving, and having a drink to discuss the questions the interviewer would ask, and how we would run things so as not to take up too much time.

"Be sure to ask about his use of animation, mixing it with live action," I said.

"Yes, already on my list," the interviewer responded.

Normally I do the interviews for the show, but our normal camera guy couldn't make it, so I was doing camera for this particular interview, giving one of the other hosts an opportunity.

After finishing our drinks and agreeing on the best way to get the whole interview done in under ten minutes, we moved back to the other bar. There was still no bartender working, but a small group of people had formed over at one of the other tables in the space. Other than that, it was still empty.

As we started setting up we realized there was music playing; more people were starting to arrive, joining the others in what looked like a wedding party. At this point, it was clear that we weren't going to be able to do the interview in that space due to the people and the noise. I went upstairs to see if there was some other out-of-the-way space we could use for the interview, when the filmmaker arrived. At the top of one of the flights of stairs, there was a nice little sitting area that didn't seem to have any people coming through. The music wasn't playing, and the window behind the bench on the landing was large and allowed for lovely soft lighting to be used.

Figuring this would work well, and heading back down the large stairwell in the center of the hotel, I could see my camera on the tripod in the middle of the lobby. There was a hotel employee angrily talking to another gentleman. The other gentleman was the one who ran the festival. The angry hotel employee was yelling at him through a perceived association with us. It was clear that the reason my camera was out there was that one of our crew was moving everything out of the room. No problem, I thought, since I had found another location anyway.

I went down and stood by my camera, waiting for the rest of the crew to join us. The two guys were about three or four stairs up the large wide staircase, and since my camera was at the bottom, I could overhear the conversation. "He needs to get that camera out of here." referring to me. "I don't know who these people think they are."

So, I turned and asked, "What is the problem. What are you getting so angry for?"

"You guys aren't supposed to be here. You didn't clear anything with me."

"Okay," I responded, "We'll move; relax."

He then turned to me fully and walked down the stairs and standing a few inches away from me, he said, "You need to leave. Get out"

"Excuse me. Why?"

"Because I told you to."

"Okay, but I still don't really understand why you are so pissed."

I get why he had a problem with us being there. We didn't check in with him in advance, and he had a wedding coming in to use the space we had started to use. And, honestly, I wouldn't have minded leaving. The weather outside was nice that day, and we could have easily done our quick interview in the large grass area in front of the hotel or the veranda. The problem I had was his behaviour. He was getting bizarrely angry over what really amounted to very little. I don't know what happened in the conversation prior to my return downstairs, but I was only gone a few minutes, and I know the other three members of the crew well enough to know, that none of them would have argued with him if he had just said, "Excuse me, sorry guys but I can't have you here. There is a wedding coming in and I need you to clear out."

We could have then responded with, "Oh sorry, we didn't know. No problem we will move. Is there another space we can use or would you prefer us to go outside?"

Two completely different ways of handling a situation. The reason I tell this story is it turned out that the angry man was the general manager of the hotel. He was the person who is responsible for the overall function of the hotel. He was the person who makes sure guests are happy. Sure, we weren't staying at the hotel, and we hadn't booked the space for a wedding, but we did spend money—not as much as a wedding, but a guest is a guest in my opinion. We were also potential customers who might have stayed at the hotel at some point.

Without calling out this hotel as an example, although I already have, employees follow the behavior of those at the top. The manager is the one who sets the example, the person who others look up to for guidance on how they should behave. This is management lesson 101 for anyone who goes into the field. So, when visiting TripAdvisor and seeing reviews saying the hotel was lovely but the service was rude, well yes, because that is where the employees learn it from, the manager. Yes, this book is about managing a manager but I hope people get a little more out of it than just that. It also touches a little on how to be a good manager. If your employees need to manage you, cover for you, work the system to get things over on you, that says something about you as a manager. In this day and age, everything we say and do can be recorded on video, written on blogs or review sites, or added to books. In his book *Tough Shit: Life Advice from a Fat, Lazy Slob Who Did Good*.

Kevin Smith devotes an entire chapter to a poor customer service experience he received from Southwest Airlines.[xii] In his situation, he retaliated by using Twitter and social media, which eventually reached higher-ups in Southwest who reached out to him to rectify the situation. In my example, by looking at TripAdvisor, I can see that the manager will often respond to comments complaining about bad service. His responses have an apology but also tend to offer an excuse. He doesn't appear interested in making the customer happy. Yes, sometimes there is a reason for bad service, and yes, sometimes the customer is not right, but also sometimes a manager shouldn't justify negative service, especially when that manager is the one setting the example of negative service.

Quite a few of the stories throughout this book relate to customer service. In life, it could be argued that every interaction we have with someone is a form of customer service. The previous example had a bad manager setting an example of bad service, which then flows downhill to the employees who see him behaving like that, and who then also provide poor service. In the previous chapter, when the manager comes out and asks the employee to create a report, and the employee responds with a yes and statement, is that any different from walking into a McDonalds, ordering a meal deal, and having them offer large fries and drink? Yes, they are made to do it because McDonald's wants that extra few cents in income, but they are still offering the up-sell in a polite manner, so that people will return to McDonalds. The general manager at this particular hotel made sure that I, and a few other people, would never stay there, and would not recommend the hotel to others, when all he really needed to do was to be polite in his interactions with us.

We all answer to someone in some way. CEOs answer to the shareholders, CEOs answer to the board of directors, and they answer to public opinion. From personal experience, I have found that the higher up in a company someone is, the more they act like they are above personal responsibility in behavior, and can act in any way they like. But in the modern world with the Internet, which provides everyone the opportunity to state an opinion on anything, it is more and more important to learn that any action we take can have repercussions, including the actions by those at the top.

A great story that my friend Andrew likes to tell goes back to a weekly meeting we had with some sales agents for Yahoo. I didn't work for Yahoo, but they were involved in a partnership with the company I was working for. The meeting started off, as usual, a bit late as we waited for the fifteen to twenty people from both companies to join. After that, we had the weekly review, and then opened it up to questions at the end. One that question directed to me had something to do with what I was working on, and I didn't have much of an update for the requester. But she was dealing with the customer directly and looking for more. I told her I would try to get her an update as soon as possible. I was doing this at the exact same time that one of my managers was emailing me about another issue. Then a person walked over to my desk asking me about a third issue, where I responded with, "No I don't have time to help you with that. I have Jennifer on the call bitching about this stupid thing, and my manager…." At that time, I noticed the guy across the desk from me waving his arms, and the manager who was emailing me running out of the office, along with others. I had forgotten to mute my phone.

As hilarious as it was for Andrew to watch this take place, I was technically in the wrong by letting myself get frustrated, and taking it out in unnecessary places. Jennifer was just asking for an update, she was my customer, swearing about her and my manager at the same time, I provided bad service to them. So later that day, as my manager had me bent over her desk with an un-lubricated fist up my ass, I took the abuse, learning a valuable lesson—not just the obvious one of muting my phone, but that every interaction we have with someone could backfire, or be taken poorly, depending on how it was delivered. A better response would have been, "Yes, I will help you with that but I need to wait until I'm done with these two things." Simple enough. Just like the guy at the hotel. I would have been saying the same thing, just not in a negative hostile way.

All of life passes from one compromise to the next. We all think we do it, we all think we are good at it, but really is very difficult to do. Now, I'm not talking about how you compromise with your wife when she wants to go to see the romantic comedy and you want the action flick—and the compromise is that you go with her to the romantic comedy and the action flick with your friends. I'm talking about the kind where neither of you fully get what you want, while both getting a little of what you want.

I was working on a project with five very opinionated people. To my left was Jerry and to my right was Brian. This situation was connected with a show that I was working on for a YouTube channel. It was one that I had helped set up, but I was attempting to step away from it and letting someone else take over. This was that first meeting with the new production manager, and as things often happen with creative people, the discussion got around to where people wanted to see the show go in the future. Jerry to my left and Brian to my right disagreed on many things during the meeting, I agreed and disagreed, as well as the others. In my mind, the meeting had gone well, yet when it was over Brian had left. We didn't know until later that he was upset about the whole thing, when he sent me a message saying he wanted to drop out of the project, and didn't like the direction the show was going in.

"Just can't get excited about where it's going. I think it's only right that I say goodbye and good luck to the show," His message read.

My response was, "What? Why? Just because things got a little heated last night doesn't mean you should leave the show. It's a good thing we were arguing about stuff. That's a sign people care and want it to be the best. And what aren't you liking about the direction?"

He wanted to take the show into a more mainstream direction, focusing more on clickbait, which made sense, since this was a YouTube show. The rest of us wanted to keep it tied to the original creation. Brian did get a lot of what he wanted during that meeting, I would even say he got most of what he wanted in comparison to the rest of the production team, but he didn't get everything. The team as a whole compromised, no one really fully received what they wanted but the show as a whole got better. The new production manager did a perfect job of taking the lead and saying, "these are the areas that we will focus on now, and we can revisit some of those other ideas later."

It is unfortunate that Brian felt the need to leave the show, but any time we work in an environment with multiple people, who are all looking at things from different points of view, so we have to be willing to look at the big picture, and make some compromises. What happens when we don't? We end up with a Trump-style presidency… haha.

Sorry, too soon? Okay, when we don't compromise we end up working alone. How about that? Brian is off doing his own thing now, and good luck to him, but I think the show would be better off if he had stayed on and been more willing to compromise.

Bad Managers

Ask yourself these questions:
1. Does your manager make you better at your job or worse at it?
2. Does your manager want to see you move ahead or do they use you to move themselves ahead?
3. Do you avoid your manager as much as possible or look forward to your interactions with them?

Depending on your responses to these questions you either have a good manager or a bad one. If you are one of the lucky ones who has a good manager, someone who wants you to be the best you can be, you are lucky. It is possible, however, that since they are so good, they will move on to bigger and better things. With a quick change in management, you might end up with a bad manager, so how do you deal with the bad one? It can be a challenge to manage a bad manager.

People in organizations tend to take their cue about how things work, not from published goals and the team vision, but from the unwritten behavior of those in positions of authority. It is important as a manager not only to set the team dynamic in published presentations and a link to the HR website, but through behavioral cues. Often, bad managers are not aware of their failings, and as employees, it is not our responsibility to make managers aware of them. As adults, we have reached the point where we are who we are, and not much is going to change that. Politics is something everyone talks about, but when was the last time you or the person you were debating changed their mind on a political subject? Very damn rarely, one would imagine. That is why, when working with a bad manager, don't bother trying to change their habits, just figure out how to work with them as best as possible. Or, work around them.

    Most people will try to avoid the bad manager as it can be easier to avoid problems sometimes than confront them. However, when it comes to others, your association with that manager could hurt your career, especially in situations where the manager messes up and you get the blame for it. The key to dealing with a bad manager isn't necessarily to avoid them, although that might work on occasion, but to find ways to get that manager working for your benefit instead of against it. How you deal with this will vary depending on the type of bad manager you have, so let's highlight a few of the major ones. First and foremost, we need to identify the bad managers and classify them. This will influence the best way to deal with them so that you will have the most success possible.

Workaholic Manager

This one will send emails in the middle of the night, and wonder why you didn't respond until the next day. A workaholic is the one whose life revolves around work, and expects yours to as well. This is my least favorite type of manager, as I am a strong believer in work-life balance, and that work is for the purpose of paying for the life outside of work. A bad workaholic might have a bad life outside of work, making work the best part of life for that person. Perhaps the workaholic types don't realize that they don't need to work so much to be successful, and maybe they think they are doing you a favor by expecting you to work as much. Also, a workaholic might be the product of a specific culture. Some countries are more focused on working while others are less so. It is possible to work with a bad workaholic, it just takes a bit of setting appropriate boundaries.

How to Manage

There are two ways to manage this type of person. The first is to make them think you are working at all hours and care as much as they do about the job. The second option is to make sure they understand that you aren't that type of person, and that you won't be responding to emails in the middle of the night. A good manager who is a workaholic will allow you to set this boundary, but a bad one won't. We will get into working with a good workaholic in the next chapter. When it comes to bad workaholic managers, personally, I've always pushed back, preferring my personal life over my work life. But not everyone is like me. And I'm not saying everyone should be either, because one thing I have learned by pushing back on a bad workaholic manager, is that it tends to make my life harder compared to dealing with it in a subtler way.

Since we are discussing the bad workaholic manager, you will probably need to pretend to play along with their working all hours behavior. The biggest problem people have with not respecting others' time is setting up meetings at odd hours. If your manager sets up a meeting at seven in the morning or seven at night, instead of during reasonable hours, accept the invitation but don't go. It's easy to say "I forgot about it since it's at such an odd time," or "I missed the reminder. Sorry." They will accept that, you won't have to go, and next time they might set it up for a reasonable time, knowing that you might miss it. This can backfire, however, as your manager may perceive you as not being a person who manages your schedule well. Another good option for this, if they do it often, is to book something else during the times you don't want to meet. Outlook will show the subject, so make sure it looks important. It is even better if you have a peer who you can book the meeting with, so that you can cover for each other. That way the manager will go to book a meeting with you and your calendar will show a booked. Many bad managers won't care, and send the invite anyway, but you can always decline it due to a "scheduling conflict". I used to have a manager who would often book meetings during lunch. My solution was to schedule a twice-weekly sync during lunch time with a friend of mine. That would at least give us two days a week for lunch that we could avoid getting booked by our manager. If you are invited to a meeting that doesn't require you to talk a lot, dial in from the drive home. I once dialed into a meeting from a rest stop on the side of the highway. It was a Friday and I had taken a work-from-home day, but really it was a travel day for a long weekend. The only thing I had to do was dial into a meeting and respond to a few questions, and then I was able to continue down the road with my manager assuming I had worked from home all day.

If your workaholic manager sends emails at odd hours, don't give into the temptation of replying to them via your phone when at home. This just sets a bad precedent and they then start to expect it. Send the email during normal hours but say you put it on a delay so that it would not arrive until after your manager got to work, because you don't want to bother them at night. They might feel guilty about doing it to you, and it gives you time to reply in the morning when you get to work. If you want to reply or email right away, look at getting a bot. Modern technology is getting advanced and AI assistants are a thing that you might consider.

Suck up Points

A way to make it look like you are the same type of person as your manager is to get e-mails ready and set a send delay on them in Outlook. Have them go out at odd hours, even though you are not working at those hours. Your manager will think you are as hard working as they are, even though you are not. If there is a day that you will be working late for some other reason, set up a meeting which shows them you are still at work. Or just happen to walk past his or her office so that you are noticed working late in the office.

Micromanager

We hear a lot about this type of manager. It is interesting that everyone says they hate this type yet they still exist. They are the control freaks that have a hard time letting go, and often don't even realize they are like this. Have you ever heard of anyone saying that they are micromanagers? No, of course not, micromanagers usually think they are doing a good job. In fact, the micromanager sometimes has the best of intentions, in the sense that they are actually trying to help people, but don't realize how they are undermining people and reducing enthusiasm for the job.

Managers get work done, managers don't do work. This sounds a little odd, but the role of a manager is to motivate those who do the work, and to do it well. Micromanagers have a tendency to be the type of people who do the work, because they think that their way is the right way to do things, which is counterproductive to what they should be doing. Not only does it demotivate the worker by making them feel second-guessed, it creates more work where there doesn't need to be.

On the other hand, sometimes, people need to be micromanaged. It's an unfortunate nature of the business, but if you are experiencing an issue with being micromanaged it might be worth taking a quick look at yourself. I worked with a guy who we will call Guy. We were on the same team when the manager changed. The new manager came in and began to micromanage him—at least from his point of view, he was being managed that way. Since we were in the same role and I wasn't being micromanaged, I told him to take a look at the way he worked. I could see throughout the day the amount of time he was spending on Facebook or other non work-related things, and I could see that it wasn't the manager that was the issue. This individual was used to the previous manager, who allowed him to get away with a lot, compared to the new manager who could see the lack of performance and had to step in and do a little micromanaging. The key to doing this, if you are a manager—and for some odd reason you are reading this—is to know when to step back. Maybe you need to manage individuals a little closer, but maybe you also need to know when to step back and start letting them do their work. Micromanaging rarely benefits the team involved. If a person is slacking and needs a more hands-on approach, maybe it is because they don't feel challenged in the role.

Remember that kid in school who acted out a lot, and would usually get punished for it, and was then forced to conform with everyone else? What if that child just found everything boring, and needed more of a challenge at school and an opportunity to excel. That child eventually grows up and joins the workforce. They may not need to be micro-managed, they may need an opportunity to outperform.

How to Manage

The best way to deal with a bad micromanager is to micromanage them back. When they give you a task, take notes from the task and send them it to the manager. Then, when they later question you on it, you can refer back to the meeting notes you sent. By doing this often, the manager will either step back a bit, or give clearer instructions. Another key way of dealing with the micromanager is to flood their email box. If they are constantly asking for updates, checking your work etc. you can start cc'ing them in on every email you send. That way they can have the updates without bothering you. The micromanager in most cases will eventually get tired of the time spent micromanaging, and as time goes by they will back off as they begin to trust you. It can take time, you have to be patient and refrain from informing them of how annoying they are.

If the micromanager is the type who does work for you, I would say sit back and let them, that is one benefit of having a micromanager. After all, you are getting paid either way, and if they are doing the work for you, great. When possible, be sure to take credit for it of course. Since they are doing your work it will have your name on it. Use the time to sit back, and enjoy watching cat videos on YouTube. Note that you won't be able to do this for long, so you better hope that the manager moves into another role—or you might want to start looking for a new role yourself.

Suck up Points

Be sure to thank them for the input they add to whatever work it is they are butting their nose into. Everyone appreciates being thanked for helping out and offering advice. More importantly, tell them how much you appreciate that they don't micromanage. Since managers rarely believe that they do this, they will appreciate the feedback, feeling good about themselves. As Dale Carnegie told us, when we thank someone for something we want them to do and praise them for it, they will be more likely to do it again.[xiii] As in "thank you for allowing me to get this done without watching over my shoulder the whole time." They will be less inclined to watch over your shoulder.

The Negative Boss

Interestingly enough, you will encounter the negative or quick-to-anger boss more often as you move higher in the company. Even if you are not moving up within the company, you might encounter this type of person when you deal with those who are higher in the company. My theory is, that as someone moves up the corporate pyramid, the notion of self-importance increases, resulting in situations where they are less likely to be held accountable for negative behavior. Steve Jobs is a well-known example of someone, who as the head of Apple, would frequently yell at those he felt were not performing at the level he wanted. Unfortunately, we give him a pass on this because he took Apple out of its slump, as well as giving us the iPhone and other Apple products that people love obsessively. I'm not arguing that he wasn't a brilliant person, but to be brilliant doesn't give one the right to disrespect those in lower positions within a company.

Luckily, most of us won't move up high enough on the corporate ladder to report to the Steve

Jobs types, so we don't have to worry about that. But we will report to a lot of people who want to be Steve Jobs and think that by behaving like him they can become him.

Another reason that a manager might behave in a negative way is that they think by putting others down it makes them seem better. A working relationship is, in many ways, like a non-work relationship. Imagine a couple, where one person in the couple is putting the partner down, or getting mad at them for no reason. This situation is often attributed to the negative person trying to put themselves above the other, in a similar way to a work environment.

How to Manage

Dealing with this boss type is a little more difficult because you can't call them out for being jerks, and if you do, that is when you risk the wrath of this boss type. The best way to deal with the angry boss is to become their best friend. Yep, kiss-ass and talk to them about whatever annoying subject they want. Be buddies. For some reason, the dick-head manager is much less likely to be a dick to you if they like you personally. I don't know why, it just is. They say smiles are contagious, so smile. And when your manager is chewing out someone else, don't come to that person's defense. If they want to stand up to the jerk of a boss let them. By letting someone else take the wrath, it allows you to move ahead of that person on the promotion scale. My strategy in the past was always to stand up to this managerial type, and it usually resulted in me having a much worse day than they did. Over time I learned to do the opposite and not stand up to them, but to stay out of their way. I learned to let others take the brunt of their wrath over a failed project or something not working the way they wanted it to work. It was just like a war zone, and when the bombs and shrapnel are flying in the air, the smart soldier ducks down and gets the hell out of the way. The dumb one runs in head first. Yes, he might be a hero, but a dead hero is still dead. In the corporate world, it's much better to be an executive's golf buddy than to be on that executive's shit-list.

A good manager knows that people respond better to positive reinforcement over negative behavior. Not only does criticizing someone create resentment, that person is less likely to outperform for that manager. Criticism not only creates resentment but can also demoralize the employee. They might be great at what they do, but when they get to a point of not caring, with low morale, they are on the verge of leaving the company. A negative manager usually doesn't realize it is their behavior that is the cause of a high turnover rate within the team. So, don't try to be the one to inform them of this. Let them think that behaving like a jackass will move them ahead in the company. If it does, great, because that gets them away from you. If they don't, then it won't matter to you, because you will be the one that the jerk boss turns to in order to complain about not getting the recognition they think they deserve. Then you can use that information to progress your own career.

Suck up Points

Sucking up to the angry boss will involve taking it in the pooper just a bit. If they are ranting at you just bend over the desk and take it in agreement. They will often respect you more for it. Better, though, is to find that common interest. Do they like golf as some big-time wannabe managers do? Then take up golf and work on your game. When they talk about some book they just read on how great Steve Jobs was, find that book and read it as well, telling him or her how great you also think Jobs was. This is where the chapter on kissing ass comes in handy.

The Indecisive

We have all dealt with this type at some point I imagine. This is the manager who can't make a decision, and consequently, nothing gets done. An example someone gave me is her manager, who would often take a poll among the team before deciding on a plan of action. The team was consulted with the question "Should we do this or this?" This is fine, but it falls on the manager to actually make the decision based on that feedback. The problem arises when the team members disagree and the manager doesn't make a decision.

My personal experience with an indecisive manager happened when I was on a team which had monthly goals, and if we met them we would be given money for team events. Prior to the manager taking over the team, we would usually do whatever the majority wanted. This particular manager required everyone to agree on the event. If someone didn't want to do paintball or wine tasting, then we didn't do anything at all, often going months without a team outing, and letting that money go to waste.

How to Manage

This manager type is actually reasonably easy to manage. Since they are so concerned about making everyone happy, all you have to do is to get everyone on board with your idea in advance. For a team outing, talk to your peers in advance, saying something like, "A few of us want to do paintball. You agree to go along with that this month, and next month we will agree with your wine tasting." And let's say the person really doesn't want to do the paintball. That is no problem, all he or she has to do is cancel last minute due to a family emergency, such as the husband has to work, so someone has to stay home with the kids. Since it's already scheduled, the manager isn't going to ruin everyone else's day, and of course, since he or she doesn't want to make people angry, the paintball will proceed one person short.

You can also make decisions for this type of person. Often, they know they are indecisive, so someone stepping in and taking care of the decisions is a good thing, especially for contracted workers. Contractors are generally hired for a specific project, then once it is done the contract ends. But, thanks to the indecisive manager, changes will continually be made, which extends the contract.

Suck up Points

Sucking up to this is relatively easy as well. The indecisive manager hates making decisions, so if you can step up and take care of some of the decision making, then they are happy. Just don't do it in an obnoxious way.

Simply Incompetent

This type is the stupid boss, the person who knew the right people in order to move ahead, or just plainly doesn't understand the job, but somehow managed to get it anyway. It can be hard to refrain from speaking condescendingly to this type of person, especially if you are a developer type who already thinks you know more than everyone else. Maybe it is just my experience, but I have found the large companies are more likely to have incompetent people in managerial roles. My assumption is, that in larger companies it is easier for them to slip through the cracks and move up the chain. Someone who is incompetent will give you instructions that don't make sense, they will throw you under the bus, they will also usually end up shooting themselves in the foot at some point as well. So, fight the urge to point out the flaws in everything they say. A nice thing about the idiot manager is they will usually get noticed for it as they move up in a company. Not always, but usually.

How to Manage

Working for an incompetent boss can be to your benefit or detriment, within the company, depending on how you handle it. If you are like me, it is usually the latter as I am prone to pointing out all the problems with everything my managers said, which didn't hurt their career as much as it did mine. To deal with an incompetent manager, I recommend avoiding them as much as possible. Just sit back, do your job, and wait for them to screw up enough times for their manager to take care of the problem for you. Another method of dealing with the incompetent boss is to think of them as the employee, and you as the manager. You can take control of your one-on-one meetings, you can run the agenda, and you can discuss the important stuff. When they give you poor instructions for something, be sure to get them written down in an email. That way, when you do what they wanted, and it doesn't work out, you can cover your own butt referring to the emailed instructions that you followed. With this strategy, as they continue to mess up, and their manager becomes aware of it, you are covered.

The Bully

No discussion on bad managers would be complete without mentioning the bully. The guy who used to push people around in school made it into the corporate world, and now continues to push people around. This is the one that thinks he can do whatever he wants, say whatever he wants to say, and get away with it. The problem is that he usually does get away with it. This is another personality type that we see more as someone moves up in a company, because as they get more authority, there are fewer people who can push back.

How to Manage

There are two ways to deal with a bully, and that is to stand up to them or to befriend them. We all learned that valuable lesson in school, that if we let the bully push us around he will continue to do it. As an adult he behaves the exact same way. I would always push back; I had no patience for bullies in school or as an adult. In the corporate world it can be hard to push back, because they are the boss and we have to put up with them. So a better solution is to befriend the bully—once again, just like the kid in school. The bully bossed his buddies around, but he didn't actually bully them. Since he is your boss, you are going to be bossed around anyway, so you might as well be a friend who is bossed around, rather than someone who gets bossed around and also pushed around.

Suck up Points

Don't question their decisions. A bully hates to be questioned. So instead of questioning the bad decisions, just keep your mouth shut. Bullies tend to not stay around long, because no one likes to work with them. Sit back, keep your head down and wait for them to move along. It is not really sucking up, but it is avoiding getting on their bad side.

Real World Example

I was sitting in the conference room talking to a few of the managers that had already assembled. We were discussing usual the general nonsense that people talk about before meetings begin.
"Who are you and why are you here?" the director of my organization said to me as she walked into her manager meeting.

"I'm Milo and you asked me to attend this meeting last week."

What makes this person a bad manager, besides not knowing the people who work for her, or the meetings she had with those people a week prior? She was someone who moved up, not through talent and management ability, but because she just happened to be in the right place at the right time. She was one of the people who had been hired at a lower level in a growing organization, so that as the organization expanded, she moved up the ladder based primarily on her longevity with the company.

After her warm greeting upon entering the room, I didn't respond with "I'm Milo and you invited me, you stupid cow," (although I wanted to), I continued telling her "And you wanted me to come and present this SharePoint redesign project to your managers. By doing this I was reminding her of our previous conversation. She remembered, or at least pretended to, and the meeting continued. This meeting also reaffirmed what I already knew about this particular manager, that she was useless and simply incompetent.

There were a few ways I could have dealt with her. I could have started making my presence more prominent to her in other meetings, and in hallway conversations. She would have then known who I was, and it might have paid off for me at some point in time. Another option was to spend my time sucking up to people who I could actually stand to be around, and who could also could benefit my career. I chose the second option. I'm sure many people would pick the first option. In this example, it didn't matter much, because she was removed from me far enough in the chain of authority, that I didn't need to have much interaction with her on a daily basis. Eventually, as often happens in many corporate environments, she moved to another role, and a much better person came in to take her place. I categorized her in the strategy of just avoiding and staying out of her way until she left. Sure, I could have made myself more known to her, but to what end? I would have gone home frustrated at dealing with her, and lacking self respect for sucking up to her. Luckily, by waiting it out, the large company I was working for moved her somewhere else, and I never saw her again.

There is another option when working with someone like her, and that is to leave, and move to another company, or another role within the company. One nice thing about the large corporate environment, is that it provides the ability to move around, while still retaining tenure and other benefits.

As someone who might be in a situation of possible job change, you need to ask yourself, is it worth it? It is easy to become complacent in our work. We might look at the paycheck and that fancy TV we sit in front of each night exhausted, as we forget about the day's work we have just completed. We think about how much we will enjoy retirement someday, looking at our 401k contributions and stock vesting awards. as we count down the days until it all ends. Yet changing roles can still provide a nice retirement plan. The health benefits of working in a positive environment include more energy, less risk of illness due to stress, and even if you are concerned about the salary, studies show that changing companies is one of the best ways to increase your salary. In fact, as per an article in *Forbes*, if you stay in a company longer than two years, you will be paid less than you would if you were to leave, and do the same job elsewhere. The reason for this is that most companies' average wage increase is around 3% of your current salary, while in leaving the job altogether, you can negotiate a new wage with a higher increase.[xiv]

The Intimidator

Similar to The Bully we have The Intimidator is your alpha male personality type. The power manager. The one who wants to be the boss and prefers to fight his way to the top. He enjoys the fight, and gets pleasure out of watching people cower at his greatness. In generations past he would have been the warrior on the field wielding an axe, rejoicing in the slaughter. However, in the modern world, with most actual battles being fought on foreign soil, the axe wielding marauder is stuck pushing his way through the hallways of a modern office building.

Also, we have the blatant sexism of this archetype. When women behave in an intimidating way, they are more likely to be called out for their behavior and shamed for it. It isn't viewed by society as a sign of strong leadership – for women, more often than not it is seen as proof of them being unstable and too emotional.

When it comes to making business decisions, this is often not the person who should make choices for everyone. Since they intimidate their employees into submission, people will often say nothing rather than endure the wrath of the overly angry boss if they don't like what they are saying. The Intimidator is often not fully informed before making decisions that could have an impact on the business, often making a rash judgment, then when things go wrong, passing the blame for the bad decision on to others.

An example of what can happen with this managerial type is an engineering team I previously worked with. I had left the team, but heard the stories through those I kept in touch with. After I left, a new manager replaced the old one. Within the first year of his taking the role, the entire team had left by quitting or being fired. Having worked with those people, I can attest to the quality of their performances. What happened was the new boss was a jerk and if people had an issue with it, they were forced out or, if he could justify it, fired. He didn't like people who questioned his decisions or actions. He didn't like things being done in any other way than his way. And those who couldn't work like that were left as fodder on the battlefield.

Luckily, I didn't have to work for him, but I did occasionally have interactions with him since I was still with the same company. In meetings, he would regularly point out how people were wrong and how he was right and how he had no interest in hearing what anyone had to say. I know myself well enough to realize that I wouldn't have lasted long working for him. How he ended up in the position or was able to stay in it so long I don't know, as I felt that the director of the organization generally made good decisions when hiring. But as mentioned, I had left by that point so was not privy to any additional information other than what I heard through second hand conversation.

Recently I was having a conversation with someone who told me a story about working in a restaurant and the chef would often yell at him and others, calling them names and putting them down. He told me this story to show how he could brush off bad behavior by others, how he could put up with it and not let it get to him. This is not a good lesson to learn, by the way – it is letting people get away with bad behavior. The same applies to that intimidating manager on my former team. He got what he wanted as a manager through scare tactics and intimidation. The interesting thing about this is, in today's world of not being able to say anything that would offend anyone publicly, within the walls of a business people can still get away with this behavior. With a chef, they might even be given a reality TV show.

How to Manage

First, don't bother standing up to them. Yes, you can, and we often think to ourselves that if put in a similar situation, we would. That was what I was thinking when that guy told me about the angry restaurant chef he worked for. But what worked with the schoolyard bully doesn't necessarily translate to the office. They will view you as a threat to their authority and do whatever they can to remove you from the place of business. I can attest to this through an experience at an employer many years ago, when I stood up to a similar manager who was not a fan of being questioned. When I called him out for his negative behavior he didn't back down. He didn't respect me for standing up to him. Instead, he spent the rest of my time working for him making me miserable, giving me the shitty tasks and constantly looking for an excuse to make my life difficult - something he successfully achieved.

What can you do? First, try to stay under the radar. The nice thing about this person not wanting to hear anyone else's opinions is you don't have to give one. When they make bad decisions, it will hopefully fall on them, especially if the person they report to is aware of their behavior. Just try to stay out of the way when they attempt to pass the blame. For me, I like to undermine this type of person whenever possible, as I don't think people should be allowed to get away with pushing others around. Be very careful not to get caught by him and suffer at his hands. But maybe let mistakes he made or unprofessional things he said slip in casual conversation at lunch or social events, things that might be repeated to someone else. If they rage in email, be sure to keep that email as a record should you ever need it. And maybe make a reply that cc's someone else. We live in an age of technology as well, so is it possible to record something via video or audio that could slip out on an internal site or even an external one? Be very, very careful to cover your tracks on this one. It is all about subtly undermining this person's authority and showing others how bad the behavior is.

If you leave the company and do an exit interview, this might be a good opportunity to call out that individual (as long as it does not affect your references, maybe get your written reference first), and after you have left and secured a new job, write a review on websites such as Glassdoor.com.

Suck up Points

I would not recommend trying to befriend this person. Think about that schoolyard bully and his friends. Do you want to be a sidekick to Biff Tannen? I wouldn't. And if you do, then it means you want to be just like them, which means, you suck! My recommendation is to agree with everything they say, question nothing, stay out of their crosshairs, and wait until they move on or look for another opportunity yourself. Or hopefully they get caught for their bad behavior and fired.

Good Managers

Just as we have plenty of bad managers in the corporate world, there are plenty of good ones, and I would be remiss in this little advice book of mine if I didn't spend some time talking about them. I have to say that most managers are actually pretty good people—at least most I have worked for. A good company will often weed out the bad ones, leaving more good than bad in my opinion.

What is a good manager? A good manager, or leader, is someone who can articulate the vision of the team and get everyone working together in the same strategic direction. A good leader knows when to step back and when to step in, a good leader inspires confidence in those who work for him or her. A leader leads in a way that others will willingly follow.

Being able to properly motivate, being able to get the best out of others, a good manager in many ways is like a parent. Parents often think that their children are supposed to like them, and they want to be friends with the child. And yes, it is nice when our children like us, and want to hang out with us, but more important than that, is raising our children to be the best they can be. It is important to make them feel confident about themselves, to give them the skills they need in order to go out into the world without us, and to be successful in however they choose to live their lives. Being a manager is the same thing, but being liked isn't all there is to being good. When we manage others, it is our job to motivate that employee to be the best they can be, and to help them succeed. And just like a child who goes off into the world, as employees move up the within the company, we can be content that we contributed to that success.

Sometimes we can be friends with our boss, and sometimes we can't. What makes a manager good, is that they genuinely care about us as employees. A good manager wants us to be successful in our careers at the company. They have integrity, and as employees, we can trust a good manager to look out for us. In some situations, if they see we would be successful elsewhere, they will provide us with the support that we need in order to get there.

Aware Workaholic Manager

We have called out the workaholic manager twice, once in the bad manager chapter, and now, in the good manager chapter. It is possible to be both a good manager and a workaholic, if that is the kind of person they want to be. It is common for the workaholic manager to send emails from home, occasionally even in the in the middle of the night. The workaholic will often work late, come in early, and work weekends. This is sometimes okay, if they are aware of it, happy with it, and don't hold you to the same standard. Think of the manager with a newborn child. The child is crying at night; they are comforting the child, but they are awake, so they might as well send a few emails while feeding the baby and rocking him back to sleep. Nothing wrong with that, because they know you are not going to respond right away.

A bad manager would expect you to work the same hours. A good manager admits that they work odd hours, but makes it very clear that they don't hold you to the same standard. If they don't, then don't try to match them. Enjoy the fact that you can work normal hours. Let them get burnt out on the job while you sit back and enjoy life.

How to Manage

The main thing when working with a workaholic manager is not to try to match their schedule. If they are good about it, they know that you have a life outside of work, and they know that you won't be responding to the middle-of-the-night emails until the next day. Once you start, it is a slippery slope down the path of joining them on the late-night emails and conference calls. Make it clear to them that you don't work the same odd hours. Often when dealing with this manager type, I am up front and say," I work regular hours. I'll work hard and do the best job I can, but my time is my time." A good manager will accept that and support it.

Suck up Points

Don't suck up to them about being a workaholic. If you want to suck up to them, find something else to brown nose about. By encouraging them in this behavior you are acknowledging it as being okay, and if you do, at some point they might go from a good workaholic manager to a bad workaholic manager. Suck up by thanking them for not forcing you to work the same crazy hours. Tell them that you appreciate the fact that you can reply to the emails the next day, when you are in the office, rather than at home. By praising them for respecting your schedule they will be less inclined to try to get you working the same crazy hours that they do. You also have to perform during work hours. A workaholic won't expect you to work odd hours if they can trust you to get the job done during regular hours.

Hands-Off or Hands-On

Most of us know what we are doing on day-to-day basis, after all, that is why we were hired to do the job. A good manager sees this, and leaves us to do our jobs, only getting involved when they are needed. Along those lines, some of us think that we work well without our manager being heavily involved in our workload, but that might not be true. A good manager will know when they need to be involved, and when not to.

We usually say that we want a hands-off boss, someone who doesn't micromanage, and lets us do our work. The reality is that some of us need a manager who is a little more hands-on. Few managers truly understand when to be hands-off and when to be hands-on. So, if you find that your manager is a bit more hands-off with some people, but not so much with you, before you decide to be offended by it, try looking at yourself. Maybe this is one of those good managers who realizes that you need closer monitoring.

Jim was a lot like me in a lot of ways. He was very creative, he liked the outside-the-box projects, and he would get disgruntled easily if things didn't go his way. The difference between us is, at the point I met Jim I had learned a bit more about working in a corporate environment, and managing my manager. Jim and I shared the same manager for a while, and when it came to this specific one, I was able to work a little more independently that he was. Our shared manager knew that she could rely on me to produce the results I said I would. Jim, on the other hand, wanted that same leniency but whenever he was given the opportunity, rather than producing the same results, he would use it as an opportunity to chat with friends at work, or leave a bit early and come in a bit late. So, when the manager became aware of this, she had to manage him a bit more closely, and, in essence, micromanage him, to which he took offense, and continually complained about, instead of looking at the possible cause of the situation. He needed to be managed this way, whether he realized it or not at that point in his career. We could debate the method that the manager used for managing him, since he took offense to the managerial style. She might possibly have handled the micromanaging a bit differently, but sometimes, some employees just need to be offended by the manager. The reality is, she identified the employees who needed more hands-on, and the ones who could succeed with a more hands-off style of managing.

I once had a manager who was easily one of my top managers. We would have a one-on-one scheduled for every two weeks instead of weekly, because she trusted me to get my work done, and when we did meet, the updates usually revolved around how things were going, and general discussions. She felt comfortable canceling meetings with me, knowing that she could rely on me, to the point that I once went a good five weeks without having a discussion with her, and she eventually just stopped by my desk to say hi because it had been so long. Yet, when I did need her involvement in a situation, I always knew I could go to her office any time, and let her know what I needed from her. Then she would get more involved as needed.

How to Manage

It is much easier to manage this type of manager because they manage themselves. Just as they can step back and let you do your job, you can step back and let them do theirs too. But don't get too comfortable with this, even though they are good at their job, you still have to remind them how good you are at yours.

As an employee, we have it pretty easy when our manager knows the right level of involvement to have in our daily workload. The best way to manage these managers is to inform them. If they are good at being hands-off in the right situations, let them know during one-on-one sessions what you are doing, and that you don't need any additional involvement from them. If, like Jim, they are getting more involved in your daily workload, spend some time finding out why. If you see them asking for more updates from you than your peers, sit down with them and discuss it. Ask what you can do to make their lives easier so, that they can involve themselves less in your work life.

Suck up Points

Thank them for being hands off and trusting you to get your work done. But the best way to suck up to them is to continue to get your work done. The more you do that, and the less they need to be involved in your life, the higher the probability that you can use that extra breathing room to do the things you want to do, like taking long smoke breaks.

Promote Your Strengths

A good manager knows that it is better to focus on your strengths than to constantly try to fix your weaknesses. This is difficult, as it is our mistakes and weaknesses that are noticed by others, and we are always looking for areas of improvement. During interviews and annual reviews, one of the common topics is "areas for improvement," followed by details of how you can improve. Rarely do we discuss our strengths and strategies to make them stand out more. During my time in corporate life, my team received training specifically focused on finding our strengths and utilizing them to succeed, instead of focusing on our weaknesses. Generally, it is much easier to be successful when we focus on what we are good at. It also takes more energy to improve our weak areas than it does to promote our strong skill sets. A good manager will see that an employee is good at writing, and try to give him or her opportunities to write content for the company. Or maybe the employee is a great public speaker, but terrible at technical writing. Instead of sending the employee to classes in order to improve technical writing skills, a good manager will give the employee ample opportunity to get up and make a presentation to the company, or to clients, while the introverted technical writer can enjoy being in a quiet office working on content.

When I did this strength finding training it didn't tell me anything I didn't already know about myself. Interpersonal skills probably not my best skill set, as I often answer questions honestly and directly, which frustrates those who work with me, and who are looking for positive reinforcement instead of a blunt response. But, put me in an environment where I can be creative and actually work outside the box, and I will excel. And for a moment I had this attitude in a manager as well. When I made her aware that I was a bit of a writer, a project come up that involved creating and improving upon process documentation, which is something I enjoy doing. So rather than give the project to someone who would not be enthusiastic about it, she gave it to me, since I had made her aware that I would enjoy that type of work.

A good manager will stand back and let you do the job you were hired for, assuming you are a decent enough employee who responds positively to that type of management. These managers will also give you credit when credit is due, they will promote you to others, and they will show you their appreciation when it comes to review time.

How to Manage

If a manager does a good job of utilizing your strengths, it is important for you to let them know what they are. Good at coding applications? Create one and show it to your manager, so that the next time they need some cool application, you will be the first person they talk to about it.

Suck up Points

Do you enjoy it when your manager talks about how great you are at something? Well, what do you think the manager enjoys then? Talk about the things that they do well, the strengths they have. Does your manager occasionally show up with coffee for everyone? Let them know how much you appreciate them taking the time to do that, clearly, they are looking for some type of positive reinforcement for doing it. Do they have a really clean office? Point out that you like walking into the office and not having to talk over a pile of notes and folders at them.

When they give you a task that plays upon your strengths be sure to do it well. By excelling in what you are good at they are more likely to provide you with those opportunities at a later date.

A Good Person

This might seem like an odd thing to call out here but a good manager is usually just simply a good person. Yes, I believe that some people are generally good people and some people are not. A good person can also be a terrible manager. A bad person might not realize they are bad, often thinking they are good. Yet I'm sure we can think of that person we have known in life, who we can say is generally a good person. I have certainly had managers that I could say that about. Good people want others to succeed. Good people will give credit where credit is due. They will talk you up to others, assuming you deserve it, and they will give you good feedback when you need it. If they see areas for improvement they will offer to help you with those areas, and if they see areas that you are good at they will use those skills. They will promote your strength and encourage you to use them.

Luckily, I have had a few managers like this, and there were times in my life that I was not a good employee, yet they recognized the potential in me. Instead of trying to bring me down, they would still try to bring me up and help me to be successful, for which I am thankful, because in many ways what little success I had in the corporate environment, was due to finding a good manager. In general, I am not the personality type who should have ever worked in a corporate environment. As someone who has managed others, I have tried to learn from these good people and utilize the skills they taught me. If someone doesn't like to speak publicly, I'm not going to force them to do presentations, I'm going to look to other things they are good at. If it is creating content and being analytical I will look to move that person into those areas. A good manager will do this as well.

How to Manage

This is the kind of manager you can actually be friends with. This is the kind of person that you don't to talk to because you have to, but because you want to. If you have a common interest, then invite them to participate in it. We all know the best way to move ahead in a company is to be buddies with the boss, and if your boss actually happens to be a good person then all the better.

Suck up Points

Don't bother. A good person is a good person, and one of the things that makes them a good person is that you don't have to suck up to them.

Real World Example

"We are not IT's bitches" and a few other words were included in the email I had sent to one of my peers. To put this email into context, I had been having a discussion with someone from another team about a work item. It was an issue that she had worked on and she wanted me to contact one of our company's customers about it. From my point of view, I felt that she was making me do work for her that she could easily do herself, and was just trying to pass it off. We both started within the company as customer service agents before moving into our current roles. But since she had moved to an IT role within the company and my role wasn't IT related, she acted as though she was above contacting customers at that point in her career. I had considered myself somewhat of a friend to her. Along with a few other co-workers, we had spent many days getting stoned in her car during lunch breaks. So, when I was telling her I wasn't her bitch, and to do the work herself, I didn't really think it would go beyond that point. After all, she was one of my work stoner buddies.

The email did go beyond the back and forth we were having. It was a work email, and it wasn't friendly, so of course, she took it to her boss, who in turn took it to his boss, and so on. Eventually, it got to the point that my managers, as I had two at the time, were called into the office of a much higher-up. According to my managers, the big boss was so angry, that besides swearing excessively, he had spit flying out of his mouth as he yelled. It seemed a bit hypocritical of him to act in that way, considering he was that mad about me behaving in a similar way.

My two managers could have tossed me to the wolves and could easily have justified it. But they didn't. They sat in the room, they apologized on my behalf, and they took the ass-reaming for me. They, of course, called me into their shared office and relayed all this to me, but instead of berating me for my behavior, they listened to my side of story. I told them the back story. Not the getting stoned part, but that the message was intended for a recipient who I had once considered a friend, and felt I could speak more bluntly with. They could have written me up, they could have done any number of disciplinary measures for my behavior, but they didn't. By being good people in the way they handled the situation, it made me want to be a good person for them, and to perform as a good employee for them. I knew I was in the wrong, and they knew I was in the wrong, so why press it and make me bitter over it? Instead, we had a good calm discussion about it, laughed a bit at the story of the higher-up spit flying swearing type, and I learned a valuable lesson in email etiquette, without the need to be severely reprimanded for it. I would have learned the same lesson at the hands of a bad manager, but I probably would not have left the meeting with the desire to prove myself in the same way that I did with these two. In this case, I left that meeting wanting to be a better employee instead of a disgruntled one. In the previously mentioned movie *Becoming Warren Buffett*, Buffett tells a story about the time that he had run off as a youth. He didn't get far, and when his father found out, he responded with "you can do better than this". He was of a generation where beating a child was accepted, yet instead, he responded in a way that lead Warren to want to prove to him that he could do better.

When You Have Too Many Bosses

In larger corporations, one of the realities of doing business is that you might report to multiple people. Sometimes this can also happen in small business. Those of us who have worked in retail or restaurants know that we might have a store manager, assistant manager, and a bunch of shift supervisors, all vying to be the one to tell us what to do. Does your company have a manager and a few supervisors under that manager? In the corporate world we often have something called a dotted line reporting structure. In multinationals this might happen when you are working from another location. There might be the local manager, and the actual manager who is based in a corporate main office somewhere. Or, for example you might be working on a project that has a project manager, who you have items due to, or a program manager. You might not report to the project manager directly, but you have deliverables for that person, as well as the deliverables for your actual manager.

During what seemed like a brief moment at AT&T, I reported up to a great manager. He encouraged me, he supported me, he gave me good advice, and made me want to be better at my job. I did so well, in fact, that when they needed to move someone to another team, whose manager was based in California, while I was in Washington State, they asked me to change teams. I was perfectly happy where I was, but I was encouraged to make the change, as multiple people I had worked with recommended me for the new role, so I went along with the move. Yet, as with many roles, I changed from one manager type to another. I changed from a hands-off supportive manager to a micromanager. The new manager would check to see when I logged into Messenger on my computer, and if I wasn't logged in on time, she would call me to ask where I was at. This lead to me intentionally not logging in, so that when she called I could say that I was at my desk. "Oops, must have forgotten to log into messenger when I sat down, and just went straight to work." Sure, it was an immature way of dealing with this person, but it also set a standard: I may not have been online, in front of my computer, but I was still most likely working. By setting this standard, when I was at home playing video games, or having slept in, and not showing as being available, she might think that I was working, and hesitate to call me. That was my assumption anyway. I never really was able to test the theory, because shortly after moving to that team she was moved to our office, and instead of being a remote annoyance, she became a local annoyance.

My first actual in-person meeting with Carrie involved receiving a lecture for doing my job incorrectly, or, I should say that it involved lecturing me for not doing my job based on what she had been told by others. We were sitting in a small conference room, with her on one side of the table and me on the other. She was explaining to me what I had done wrong, while I was biting my tongue to avoid responding in anger or frustration.

The whole situation started when I was in another meeting, with another one of the three to four bosses I had to deal with at the time. One of them asked me why I didn't do something the way she wanted it done, and my only response was that I did what I was told to do, by the other manager. This was true, because the communication issue was at their end, not mine. In essence, one person said one thing, another said something different, then by the time it came down to me at the bottom of the chain, what the top boss actually wanted wasn't the same anymore. It was like those games we play at team building events, where we stand in a circle slowly going around whispering something into the next person's ear, then when it gets back around the wording has changed so much it barely connects to the original instruction.

Later, when I handed in the process documentation I had been tasked to write, I was informed that it wasn't what she wanted—in a negative condescending way. At that point in life, still believing the motto of treating others as they treat you, I responded in a similar, negative, condescending way. It turned out that they didn't like me pointing out the communication issues they had. Sure, my response could have been a little more politically correct. But the reality at the time was that multiple heads telling the hand what to do can be confusing for the hand, especially when the heads don't communicate well with one another.

Dealing with multiple managers can be really difficult, especially in situations like mine, where two of the people I dealt with were poor communicators, and had no problems passing the communication failure on to others.

I dealt with it by fighting back, by calling them out on their incompetence, and pointing out their flaws, just as readily as they had pointed out mine. I responded by subtly doing things that I knew would piss them off, and sometimes not so subtly.

But let's say you aren't me, that you have a similar situation, and want to deal with it properly in a positive manner. A former peer of mine, who we will call Daniel, had this situation. His actual manager was located in a different country, but Daniel's role needed a local manager. As such, he was the only person on his team to work out of our office, and he needed a manager who could assist him locally when needed, and who he could talk to face-to-face. This is a very common scenario in large companies with multiple offices.

In solving the problem of situations when one manager might come to him with one task, and the other with another potentially different task, which could be conflicting, he decided to be proactive before any communication breakdown issues could arise. He took it upon himself to set-up a communication system that allowed everyone to be aware of his workload and where it was coming from. He also made sure that he was meeting with both managers and updating both on what he was doing on a regular basis, usually in the form of a separate weekly meeting with each. So they both knew how busy he was, what he was doing, and who he was doing it for. He had one source of information, a source that each manager or project stakeholder could reference, in order to keep up to date with his progress on the project. During the meetings with each manager, he could take feedback and update his master project list, and share that with the other manager. If there was a conflict, he could ask the two of them to work it out. They could record it and then utilize that one resource for documentation. Yes, he had to have two meetings each week with two people, but the time he lost due to those 30-minute meetings, he gained back in not dealing with miscommunications and redoing work. It also gave him the appearance of a proactive problem solver.

Why did this work? The obvious answer is that Daniel took the initiative to create an environment in which he could work, but that is not the only reason. He also happened to be working with two good managers. The local manager was that local support structure when needed, and his remote manager was able to trust in Daniel to do his work without constant check-ins. Both could see that Daniel could do the work independently, and they were able to step back and allow him to do his job, freeing them up to work on other things. On a day-to-day basis, Daniel's managers were able to take his feedback, and trust that he knew what was required in order to be successful. In this case, there was a level of hands-off trust, which allowed Daniel to set the roles and responsibilities of each manager.

Daniel housed everything in a single SharePoint, with project status and updates provided in Excel and PowerPoint. The key isn't the tools, it is the process. It is taking the initiative, and managing the managers together, letting them know what is happening, and why. So, if or when, there was a communication breakdown, everything was documented, so that instead of the blame being passed on to him, he was able to show the information he was working from. Yes, the failure might still have been at his end, but by being transparent, his managers could identify communication breakdowns and correct them earlier, instead of at the end which is what happened to me.

An added benefit of this method of working is that come review time, we might have two managers speaking on our behalf in front of the upper manager or director. Daniel was able to have two good managers working for him, so he quickly moved up within the company. He did this by showing more than one person how successful he could be. Later, when it came to interviewing for a new role, he was able to go into those interviews having already proven his ability to the ones in charge, so that they knew they would be making a good hire decision.

Daniel was able to work with two people who deserved to be in management roles, and were aware that by allowing him to be successful, they would also be successful. It is possible when reporting to multiple people, that we might end up in a situation where one of those managers falls in the good manager side of the spectrum, and the other falls on the bad side. When it comes to working with multiple bosses it is imperative to know how each manager likes to work, and to interact with each one in the appropriate way. When working with one good, and one bad, manager this can be more frustrating, as you could find yourself dealing with the bad one more often than the good one.

At one point, I was working in a role that had two closely integrated teams. Technically, I reported to one person, but due to the structure of the organization, in essence I reported to two people. The one I was supposed to report to fell on the bad side of the scale, and the other, the good side. I wouldn't even say he was a bad manager, he just leaned a bit towards the incompetent side of the spectrum. Personally, I found him to be a very nice person, but his priorities were a bit off. Instead of caring about the quality of service I provided to the customers, he was more concerned that I would often have my feet on the desk when engaging in customer phone calls. Fine, it was a pet peeve of his, so I tried not to do it. But he would also do things like forget conversations that we had. He was a bit disorganized, and often messed up paperwork.

In one situation, I had been selected to participate in an exchange program, in which I would travel to one of our other centers, and spend a few days working with some of my peers who I had never met. This was before I changed roles, to one that involved too much travel, so I was looking forward to the opportunity. When it came closer to the time of the trip, it turned out that my manager had forgot to submit something that needed to be done, and which caused my trip to be canceled. This was just one of the issues I had with him, but a big one at the time.

Not really knowing how to deal with the situation, I went to the other manager, and asked if I could have a talk with her. I didn't go in there to complain about him. If I had, then I would have just come across as someone who complains about someone else—not the best way of making an impression. Instead I went into her office to ask for advice on how to deal with the situation. I told her some of the issues I was having and, being a good manager, she offered some suggestions on how to deal with it. My intent wasn't to get him into trouble with the other manager, but to get advice on how to deal with him. Because the good manager had taken the time to assist me, I was able to work on my relationship with the not-so-good-boss. I took the advice, and used it to improve my working relationship with him, even though I was still frustrated at his lack of follow-through in situations. But by reaching out to the good manager, I was able to more effectively work with the bad one. The bad manager, by the way, didn't stay with the company; soon after this conversation he left.

Since we have discussed multiple good managers and one of each, it would be only fair to discuss dealing with two bad ones. In this scenario, we will use the example of Steve; he and I instantly hit it off when we started working together. We had similar views on the world, common interests, and we are both extremely motivated, while also trying to do as little as possible. I know this seems at odds, but when it comes to the job, we were both are very motivated to make it as successful as possible, yet when others aren't as motivated as us, or push back, we get frustrated and instead, just sit back and watch movies all day on our laptops.

Steve and I reported to the same manager at a couple of points throughout our careers. While working together, our manager changed, and Steve didn't get along as well with the new one as our previous one, while I got along with the new one fine. As time went on, Steve's working relationship with her got worse, and it affected his performance reviews, as well as his motivation in the role.

Eventually, he decided to take this to the other manager we reported to. The mistake he made was in the way he did this. Instead of going for a nice, casual chat, and asking for advice, he went to complain. He sent emails complaining, and instead of that manager looking at the situation from Steve's point of view, Steve now had two managers who he had managed to offend. Personally, I found both the managers great to work with, but Steve didn't, and in essence, he ended up with two bad managers. In this situation, there really isn't much anyone can do. It is possible to try to repair the relationship, but once an employee gets put on the bad list, it is really hard to be taken off. Steve ended up leaving the company and going to a smaller startup, where his style of working mixed better with the nimble startup mentality.

When it comes to working with multiple managers we might get lucky like Daniel, who was able to report to two great people, and achieved success through the experience. Or we might work with one good one and one bad like I did. I could have let myself get frustrated, and truthfully, I often did, but in the end, I stuck it out. I maintained my working relationship with the good one, and did the best I could with the bad one. Since the bad one left in the end it worked out for me. I could just have easily reported to two bad people; that makes the situation harder to deal with, and usually results in the employee leaving, as it did with Steve.

Inside the Box

Yes, I know, every company says they want outside-the-box thinking, but let me tell you, outside–the-box thinking is baloney, you should ignore that idea. Outside the box is only allowed by people in positions of authority. For most of us in the lower positions of the company, we should think inside the box, while making it sound like we are thinking outside the box. Outside-the-box thinkers make waves, and we don't like waves in the corporate world. Waves represent change, and change coming from worker bees can be a bit much for some executives to handle. They like to be the ideas people, the ones who innovate. Employees shouldn't make waves, they should make stuff happen, stuff that someone else came up with. I know this sounds a bit pessimistic, but as with anything, there are exceptions to the rule. In the corporate world, however, we usually don't care about the exceptions, we care about the majority.

Don't believe me? Look at the film industry for example. The studio system for making films is a large corporation. The executives at the top hire producers to make films that make money. They don't hire a producer to make a box office flop. Often, those executives have no actual experience in the film industry, they are rich people who have experience running companies and making money. At no point do they think it is not okay to make money on a project. They look at how much the film will cost to make, what they think it will make at the box office, and then make a decision on whether or not to produce it. What do we have in Hollywood at the moment? Every few months we have a comic book hero saving the world from the most recent comic book bad guy. We have old TV shows being turned into cheesy comedies, and we have movies that have already been made, being made again or re-booted. Why? Because the public goes to watch those films. The film industry looks at the past performance of movies, and then makes a decision based on how much that same type of movie will make the next time. If a movie made money before, there is every chance it will make money again, especially with movies that have name recognition (franchises). Star Wars anyone? Most movie studios look at spreadsheets, and the stars they can secure for the film, then they decide to move forward with the project, based on the assumption that people will go to watch the movie. And they are often correct. The big budget action flick with the big-name actor makes more money than the small indie film. The indie film might have a better story, but box office receipts don't lie.

In the corporate world of technology, pharmaceuticals, or car manufacturers, they do the same as the film industry. They look at what has made money in the past, make some slight changes, and re-release it. The EpiPen is an example. The drug that goes into the EpiPen can be produced generically. The injector pin, on the other hand, is a patented product owned by one company. That company can raise the price of the pin as much they want in order to make money from the product. Sure, they could share the patent with other companies to make the injection pin as well, it would be a benefit to the world, to people with allergies, and society as a whole. But drug companies aren't formed to benefit society, they are formed to make money for shareholders.

Is the drug company going to spend time and resources thinking outside the box on how to distribute this life-saving device to others cheaply and efficiently? Of course not, they are going to remain in that box, owning the patent on the product, and lobbying Congress to make sure that an alternative outside-the-box version isn't made by other companies. Unless of course, they can own the patent on the Star Trek-style injector. But, do you think that the low man on the ladder would be the one to come up with the idea? Nope, the higher ups in the company are the ones who decide what should happen. Then the guy at the bottom is the one tasked with making it happen.

I'm a Ford motor company fan, and the Ford Mustang is a pretty cool car in my opinion. But, is the new Mustang all that much different than the original one? No, it's not. The original is cool, so they make a new one that is styled like the old one. It doesn't have an electric engine and it isn't all that much different than the original, simply because people want it that way. Apple is the most profitable company in the world. Yes, Apple does occasionally come out with something innovative, but it's not really new. The iPod wasn't an original idea. The mp3 player had been out for years. All Apple did was make it super user-friendly and look cool. They took the cell phone, which we already had, paid for some patents owned by other companies to make it look good, added easy-to-use apps, and suddenly we had the iPhone. Is the latest iPhone all that different from the first version? It might be larger or smaller, it might be lighter, it might have more memory and added functionality, but it is basically the same thing. Yet people line up around the block on the first day of release to get one. Are they buying something that is new and original? Are they getting something that some engineer came up with that is completely new and outside the box? Nope, they are buying it because it's cool, and because it was developed inside the Apple box. The Apple that knows what works and how to get people to buy the phones. Another example is video game companies who make a game, then release variants of the same thing over and over. *Call of Duty* has more versions than I can think of. Each game is basically the same as the previous version, only with a story that is a little different, better graphics, and maybe a new weapon of some kind. One takes place during

World War II and the other on a modern-day battlefield.

We can't fully blame the executives for inside-the-box thinking by the way. The consumer is to blame as well. Just like the consumer that watches the cookie cutter movies that studios release, it is the consumer demand that dictates what the companies give us. Microsoft released Windows 8, which was a drastic change from the previous versions of Windows, and the public hated it so much that the company quickly started working on the next version, Windows 10, returning functionality from previous versions of Windows. Look at mobile phones as another example. Yes, Microsoft was late to the game, but did they release a phone that was different in the design from an iPhone or Android phone? Yes, it was a bit different but the consumer wasn't interested in the Windows Phone. How about Betamax? By most accounts, Betamax was better than VHS. The electric car is another example. The first one was released in the early 1900s, but people wanted petrol powered vehicles. It wasn't until recently that we started to see a demand for the electric car, and that is only because a company took the old technology and packaged it in a way that made people want it.

The reason for all of this is the people who make decisions, and the people who work for those who make decisions being made to work inside the box. To be successful, they do it in a way that makes people think they are going outside the box. How creative of PlayStation to let its customers re-buy old PlayStation games that can be downloaded, since the PS4 isn't backward compatible, even though they could have made it that way, as they did with previous versions. They imply that they came up with an outside-the-box solution to allow people who want to play old games on the PS4, but really, it's just selling the same games to us again in a different format. Hardly outside the box, but it sure makes someone look good to have come up with the idea.

When looking to move ahead and stand out, don't get creative with your outside-the-box thinking. Change scares people, and the larger the company, the scarier change becomes. When coming up with innovations that will move the company forward and get you recognized, promoted, or a call-out at that next awards ceremony, don't get risky. Take a rock, clean it off, paint a turtle on it and call it a pet rock. That's outside the box, and will get you a nice big bonus at the end of the year for your creative thinking. If you truly want to be an outside-the box thinker, dust off your money-raising hat, fill out the patent forms, and get that startup company of yours registered as a business.

There are additional advantages to working at an inside-the-box company, because you are also working within the system. For example, are you in the process of updating your resume? Don't do it at home or during your free time, even if you are looking outside the company. Updating a resume is work-related, so do it at work. If asked, say that you are looking for internal positions. If your company doesn't offer much vacation time, but also offers sick time, use it up. Most companies that have separate sick and vacation time don't let the sick time roll over to the next year. If the sick time is a use-it-or-lose-it offering then use it, especially on a Friday or Monday when you'd like a three-day weekend.

I once made the mistake of not using my sick time properly, and learned the lesson for it. My job, at the time, was delivering software releases. I was working on an internal tool which was scheduled to be released on a Saturday night / Sunday morning. Sunday was often the day for releases, as the calls into customer service were lower, thus reducing the impact on the call centers and engineering team should it not work, and they needed to roll back the release. One thing I learned during my time at that particular mobile phone service provider, was that releases never happened on time. In fact, the entire time I was there I don't think a single upgrade happened as initially scheduled. I had to cover for a system release that had been repeatedly pushed back, interfering with almost every weekend that summer. That meant no camping trips or weekends out of town, because the release was always scheduled for a Saturday night rollover to Sunday, and I needed to be available. The release was pushed back numerous times until it got to a weekend that I did have something planned, a trip to New York. My girlfriend at the time was over for work that week, and we had talked about taking a long weekend, with me flying over for a visit.

Instead of pretending to be sick, which is what I should have done, I asked my boss for that weekend off and a couple days afterwards. I made it clear that my peers on the team had the same knowledge of the product as I did, and they could easily cover for me. The request was made on the assumption that the release would not happen that weekend either. We will call my boss at the time Christy for the purpose of this chapter. I asked Christy if I could have those days off. She wasn't the kind of manager who could make decisions on her own, so she took it to her boss. They both decided the answer was no, I couldn't take those days off. We argued over it, but of course, I lost and didn't go on the trip. At that point, I had shot myself in the foot. I had plenty of sick time available, but since I had already argued about the trip they would have known I was lying. So, I was stuck in town on a weekend that I could have been touring around New York for the first time.

As you can probably guess, the release was postponed, and I could have gone on the trip anyway. The postponement notification went out a couple of days before the scheduled release date, which was too late to book a flight. And to add icing on the cake, my boss at no point apologized or expressed sympathy about not allowing me to go on a trip, and forcing me to stay home for a system release that didn't happen.

The lesson here is very clear, if you are not 100% positive that you will get approval for the time you want to take off work, call in sick and use that as vacation time. The sick time is available, and often it expires at the end of the year, so use it or lose it! Oh, and since the chapter is about thinking inside the box, the other lesson here is, don't make waves, work within the system, yet be sure to work the system while you are in it.

Backstabbing

Since office politics involves making you look good while making others look bad, I would be remiss if I didn't have a chapter on the subject of backstabbing. We are just politicians, but on a less national scale. And if there is one thing we have learned about politics it is that part of making yourself look good is making the others look bad. Personally, I have a hard time with this, even when it comes to people I don't like, mostly because I have a strong sense of morality, and I am friends with a lot of my co-workers. As anyone who has ever worked with me can attest, if I have a problem with you I will not be slow about letting you know about it face-to-face, usually in a direct and clear manner, which gets me into trouble sometimes. But that is me, and this book is for you.

You might be thinking to yourself that you don't play in the dirty world of office politics, and internal backstabbing. That is fine if you don't, but it is possible that the guy in the office next to yours does. Even if you don't intend to get involved in this behavior it might be worth keeping an eye out for those who do, so as to be aware, and to know how to respond. Has someone had a conversation with you while speaking negatively about someone else? Does that make you think they won't do the same when speaking to someone else about you?

Remember from the chapter on bad managers where we talked about the simply incompetent manager? If you and your co-worker are reporting to this type of person, be aware that it might be easier for you or your peer to behave in a sabotaging manner towards others. An incompetent manager might not see this behavior for what it is, or even if they do see it, they might not know how to respond to it. The bad manager might also be the backstabber themselves. We have the term "thrown under the bus" for a reason, usually because the bad manager has no problem tossing others under the bus in order to make themselves look good.

I have seen backstabbing happen enough to know that if you do it right, you will look good, the other person will look bad, and you will be rewarded for it. If you do it incorrectly, you will be the most hated person in the office, and that reputation will follow you for the rest of your time in that company. People talk, after all. Okay, maybe not the whole time you are with the company, and maybe not the most hated, but the lesson is: don't get caught.

So how do you jab that knife in the back of one of your peers? One way is to poison the waters of opinion about them. Be really careful about how you go about this, because even though, in this instance, you might look good, that person you stab in the back might remember it, and someday end up in a position

of authority over you. But backstabbing is an effective way of moving ahead, and looking good.
Backstabbing types love to put others down while making themselves look good. This means that as you are talking about how great of a job you are doing, while practicing the self-promotion techniques, you occasionally slip in a word about that other person who isn't quite as great as you are.

A good way to poison the waters about someone is to take advantage of the fact that people love to gossip, especially team admins and secretaries. When you are being buddies with the team admin and having a smoke outside, you can tell a story— in confidence of course—about that time your peer unzipped his pants and threatened to show his junk to one of the girls in the office. Remember how you are now golf buddies with that asshole boss who yells at everyone? Well, how about the next time you are on the golf course or at the bar after the game, having a drink, tell him that funny story about your adversary cursing about the company to a client. Or tell that story they told you about the time they got drunk and passed out in the men's room of the bar. Clearly, the person has no self-control and shouldn't be trusted within the company. When telling this story be sure to tell it just as a funny story, don't tell it with the intent of ratting out the person or making them look bad, just let the casual conversation lead to the story. Since you are telling it as a casual conversation you won't seem like the jerk trying to get them in the manager's bad graces, but that manager will think of that story the next time they are dealing with that person. Of course, it's best to tell a story that is true and not made up. Perhaps an exaggerated version of the truth might work as well.

In order to get more usable gossip, you will need to be friends with the person you are backstabbing. I know this might be a tough one, since you are backstabbing the person, and this goes against your good nature. Or it might be difficult to be friendly because you don't like that person, hence the reason you are trying to discredit them within the company. But by being friends they are more likely to be open with you, and tell you things you can use against them at a later point in time. Of course, when bad things happen to that person in the company, or someone finds out about the time they plagiarized that report they wrote, it won't be because of you that it was found out, after all, you are their friend. When something bad happens to this person and they come to you, their friend, for advice, make sure you give them some 'good' advice. If they are having a conflict with someone tell them, "I wouldn't stand for that, I would totally confront them about it." Make it sound like they should aggressively confront that person. "Really, that executive was yelling so loud that spit was flying out of his mouth? That's bullshit and I wouldn't take it. You tell them to go fuck themselves for behaving like that." Make sure the advice you give sounds like it is something you would actually do, to help them feel like you would back them up when they actually do it, then when it happens, sit quietly and watch it go downhill for them.

If you ever get caught backstabbing one of your peers, play the innocent to get out of it. "Oh, I'm sorry I didn't realize you told me that in confidence. I just thought it was a funny story and that's why I repeated it." Or, when they come to you asking why you didn't come to their defense, simply say, "Oh I didn't realize you wanted me to, you seemed to have it covered yourself."

Numerous books and website articles have been written on the subject of backstabbing, so I'm not going to go into more advice on how to backstab someone. If you want more ideas, go out and buy one of those books or look at a few of the websites. My advice is to look at each suggestion logically. Some of the tips people give are not believable at all, and seem to be written more for humor than actual implementation. The key to backstabbing is being subtle about it, not going over the top.

Since we have talked a bit about what to do to others to make them look bad, what if someone else is backstabbing you? How should you defend yourself from this? Most advice books and websites say that you should follow the proper channels. This is most likely what your employee handbook would say as well. The HR department would advise you to talk to your manager. The manager would say you should talk to the person or someone from HR. The thing to note here is that no one wants to deal with these situations, which of course means you need to deal with it yourself. First off, don't go to HR and don't go to your manager.

Now, what to do? You could start off with ignoring it. Often with people who are bad at backstabbing, and if your manager is a good one, they are probably already aware of it, and it's not an issue. This is probably the least likely thing you should do. Ignoring a problem rarely ever makes it go away. And managers have better things to focus on than two people trying to make the other look bad. Managers care about results. Remember that time it burned when you peed? At first, you tried to ignore it but it eventually took antibiotics to get rid of the burn. You can also ignore the backstabber, but that burn will still be there.

Since we are near the end of this book you should have already started practicing the advice given in earlier chapters, one of which is being buddies with your bosses. Be the go-to guy or girl and be the trusted employee. If you have followed the advice, then you are already friends and confidants of managers and key influencers. So, when the backstabbing peer says something bad about you to them, they will recognize it as backstabbing, so they will only be hurting themselves, because you are buddies with the person they are talking to.

Usually, however, the backstabber gets away with the behavior and they are not called out on it.

Once they get away with it the first time, they will be more likely to repeat the behavior, which is why my advice is not to ignore the problem. Backstabbers are like bullies, and possibly they were bullies in school; once they realize they can get away with it they will continue. You have to do something that lets them know, that you know what they are up to, but do it in a subtle way. Then they might worry that you are on to them, and stop the backstabbing. Also, like a bully, when you fight back they usually back down and move on to someone else. However, unlike dealing with a bully, you can't challenge them to a fight behind the cafeteria. This is the office, so you will need to be subtler about it.

If subtly confronting them hasn't resulted in the correct results, it is time to move on to playing the same game. This might be the more immature and petty option but, as you have probably figured out by reading up to this point, the majority of what has been written in this book is a bit immature. And remember, you are already friends with the best people in the office to be friends with, so you can afford a little immature behavior.

When dealing with someone like this, be sure to document everything. Emails are great because they are written and dated records of something that happened. More than once in my career I have been able to cover myself by referencing an email conversation. Also, more than once in my career, an email record of a conversation has bitten me in the ass, such as the "we are not IT's bitches" example.

The key to backstabbing is that it is behind the person's back, and that you must not get caught. Backstabbing can be a long-term endeavor or a one-time event. For example, a colleague that acts positively in direct interaction, may consistently undermine your position behind your back with your other colleagues, bosses or with the entire organization. He may steal your ideas and present them as his own before you are able to do it yourself. He may take credit for your hard work. Or he may suddenly turn against you within a context where you were counting on the support he had promised.

Always remember to avoid revealing personal information or feelings on anything to co-workers, no matter who they are, as it can always be used against you. One of my managers was a pro at this. When it came to socializing she didn't socialize with anyone at work, and she was upfront about it. She clearly stated that her purpose in the office was one aspect, and her life outside was another, and she didn't mix the two. None of us who reported to her liked her, not because she didn't socialize, but because she was a bad manager. By not socializing with any of us, we never had any ammunition we could use against her at a later date.

Not being involved in the personal lives of the people she worked with was her strategy. It made sense, but she also came across as a bit lonely to me.

My strategy has always been the opposite, i.e., to be friends with co-workers. It was never a conscious choice, but we spend more time at work than any other place, and by making friends at work, it makes going in each day more enjoyable. Whatever you do, you should have a strategy for dealing with office politics and backstabbing. By the very nature of the corporate environment, these situations will arise, and knowing how to deal with them will make you more productive in your role, or will at least make you look more productive to others.

    I have spoken quite a bit about being friends with your co-workers, but this can end up hurting you as well. The manager I just mentioned, succeeded without making friends with anyone, so we weren't able to use anything against her. Remember, not everybody has your best interests at heart—just like the movies, "Don't trust anyone." Even when you are out with co-workers who are friends, be aware that anything you disclose could come back and be used against you. When you are involved in a team-building exercise and everyone has to tell the story of their most embarrassing moment, don't tell your actual one. Tell a story about something that is funny, but not that bad. Understand that anything said in private can easily be taken public. It is my advice to use if you want to backstab someone else, so there is no reason to believe that someone else won't do it to you. I once relayed a story about the time I went out to a gay bar with some friends, and drank so much that when I went to piss I passed out in the men's room, with my pants down to my ankles. A couple of the guys I was out with had to come collect me. A funny, embarrassing story, but not the best one to tell if you don't want to seem like a drunk who passes out in bars with piss in his hair, and who then needed someone else to pull up his pants.

At the End of the Work Week

You might be one of the rare people with a manager who recognizes you for your brilliance, without the need to continually remind them of your greatness. If so, that is great, but even a great manager, who recognizes those who work for him or her, can sometimes need a reminder. Managing your manager isn't just about pulling one over on those you work for, it is also about creating the best and most productive work environment possible. Productivity, being measured by *your* idea of productivity, even if your level is lower than that of your company. To make up the difference, that is where managing your manager comes in, by using some of the advice outlined in the previous chapters.

In most corporate environments, monkeys sitting at a computer writing code, putting together PowerPoint presentations, or whatever else it is you might do, are a dime a dozen. To stand out like a shiny new dime, you need to show the people you work for how great you are, but remember it is just a show. Since employees are a dime a dozen, don't waste all of your time each day doing as much as possible and working harder. Use your time wisely to look good while doing the least amount possible. We all know the old saying about no person lying on their death bed, ever once said, "I wished I had worked more." It is almost always the opposite: wishing they had worked less, spent more time with family and friends, and done the things they enjoyed more. Maybe for you, that is work, and through managing your manager you can do more of what you love. Most people will probably prefer to work less, and enjoy life more. I know I do, and if you are similar to me, I hope something in this book helps you to achieve that life.

I spent the majority of my time over the years working in the corporate world, not to mention the years prior to that working in retail, customer service, construction, and delivering pizzas. During those years, I have had more bosses than I can remember. Okay, if I sat down and thought about it, I could probably remember them all and even rate them if I had to. Some were good managers and some were bad. Some companies do a good job of hiring good managers and some don't. You might not have a manager who fits any of the categories mentioned in the manager types chapter, or you might have one that is a mixture of multiple types; we are all individuals in our own way, but managers often lean towards one of the archetypes described in this book. Learn from that, and find what works best for you when it comes to managing them. Use it as a starting guide.

When it comes to dealing with a bad manager, use the lessons provided by those you work with, and which are provided in books like this. We have all heard of the studies by B.F. Skinner[xv], in which he tested animals and found that those rewarded for good behavior learn much better than the ones punished for negative behavior. This applies to humans as well, and by being critical of others, we are only demoralizing the workers. Bad managers don't know that. So, don't let that person get you down. Just manage them in a way that gets you what you want from them, for as long as you have to deal with them.

Having been managed by so many people at various points in my life, I can say that I have had more failures than successes in dealing with them. That is why the examples in this book come from the real world, where I watched those who succeed with envy and scorn. The ones I have watched move ahead, rarely did so through hard work, they kissed ass, they promoted themselves, and they radiated an air of knowledge and confidence, that those in positions of authority saw and promoted. In the many years that I have worked in a corporate environment, I've gained the experience that allows me to pass this advice on to others, so that now you can be the success that I was not.

I've spent the majority of my adult life in the corporate world, working for large, and even larger corporations. In that time, I have reported to a many people, some of whom were great inspiring leaders, and others were not so great. Some managers I rarely ever saw, because they trusted my work, and others would change what they wanted me to do on a regular basis. Some wanted me to be a success, and others didn't care as long as I made them look good, and if I didn't, they had no problem passing the blame on to me. I've been friends with my managers, and I've had conflicting relationships with my managers. I've seen good and bad managers come and go. I've managed individuals and small teams myself. Friends and colleagues have come to me often over the years, looking for advice on how to deal with situations involving their managers. Throughout that time, I've given some good advice, and in that time, I've made some bad decisions of my own in dealing with managers. And throughout that time, I did one important thing, I learned, I observed and now I'm writing it down.

I've made coffee for a living, done customer support, project management, and yes, people management. I've worked for companies that have five employees and companies with over one hundred thousand full-time employees based in numerous countries around the world. Currently, I work for a company with one employee and one manager – me. Some days my manager is great, and others he's lazy and useless. The nice thing about being my own boss is only having myself to blame when things don't work out, and only myself to reward when they do. Someday that might change, and my career path will change again, along with the people I interact. What I can say for sure is, the experiences I gained while working for so many people make me that much better at whatever career I might change to someday.

When working in a high-pressure corporate environment, knowing how to work with your manager and peers will get you the most return, while helping prevent a heart attack, nervous breakdown, or walking out on the job. The job might change, the people will certainly change, but the skills required in order to be successful won't.

By learning to manage your manager, you aren't just learning how to slack off at work. Okay, yes you are, but you are also learning how to make yourself look good while slacking off. Managing your manager is also about getting the best out of your manager, so that they can get the best out of you. Or in the case of a bad manager, it is about looking good while waiting for that person to move on into another role, or for their manager to recognize how useless they are and move them out of the company.

You might be saying, "This doesn't seem like it's making my job easier, it actually seems like a lot of work." You have to meet with your manager regularly anyway; instead of dreading it, make it fun and talk yourself up. It's not taking more time out of your day, it's using the time that is available. Knowing whether you have a good manager or bad one, will make life easier, because you will know how to get them to work for you, instead of always having to stress about working for them.

My final piece of advice is, remember that your manager has a manager as well. As we all know, crap rolls downhill, a good manager knows how to deal with this crap, but sometimes they aren't good at it, and that crap ends up on you. Don't let it get you down, don't stress about it, just let it roll off your back. Most importantly, go home at the end of the day and leave work at work. We work so that we can afford to do the things we want to do, but by taking work home with us, it interferes with our quality time. I used to say when I started working in the corporate environment that I had to check my soul at the door in order to be successful, and in many ways, I believe that to be true. When I left the corporate world, I got my soul back. It was a bit tattered and shriveled, but it was mine, and I had missed it. So, if you feel you need to check it at the door, then check it, but be sure to grab it on the way back out.

If you have now finished reading this book, I thank you. If you got something from it I am glad. If you finished it and are now thinking to yourself that it was useless or not entertaining, or that I just sound like some jackass who thinks he is smart, well, I say thank you anyway, because you most likely bought this book and that's a sale for me. If you didn't buy this book then I don't care if you hated it. Now get to work!

Bonus Chapter: Office Pranks

I know there are a lot of websites with office pranks, but many of them are clearly written by people who want to do them but never would, as they are downright vicious. A few of the others you might find online, however, are actually hilarious if you do them. Since this is my book about working in a corporate environment, here are a few pranks that I have done to others, had others do to me, or seen others do to others.

Computer Pranks:

1. When someone leaves their computer unprotected/unlocked, open Outlook and change the signature they use in emails. Most people are so used to seeing it they don't even notice if a slight change has been inserted, such as changing a person's last name to something slightly inappropriate.
2. Along the same lines as changing the person's signature in an email, you can change the auto correct function to automatically change a word like "and" to "ass".
3. Hoff them. This is a term for going online and finding a Baywatch era picture of David Hasselhoff, and then setting it as their

desktop background image or screensaver. Another favorite of this one is Burt Reynolds' classic hairy chest.
4. Another fun one when someone leaves their computer unlocked is to send an email on their behalf to others. Usually this can be a simple "I love you guys", to a longer story about some embarrassing moment in their life. Be kind with this one, only send it to friends and people in the know.
5. Since most people these days have a Facebook account, they have usually accessed it from work at some point, so they will probably be logged in. Go to their page and post something, or start liking people from their profile such as Justin Beiber.
6. The best computer prank that you should do, is go to Amazon.com, and if they are logged in, search for this book and order them a copy. It's not expensive, and they will get these useful tips to use on you. Be sure to also give it a five-star positive rating while there.

Food Pranks:

1. Do you have some old cheese, fish, or other foul-smelling product? Stash it under the victim's desk somewhere or behind the computer.

2. Pick up of some of the cookie-looking dog biscuits from your local pet store, and bring a tray for your co-workers and place them in the break area. Just be sure to get the all-natural healthy ones made from products people would actually eat.

Desk Pranks:

1. Pick up a fart machine from the local gag store and tape it under a chair or desk. Hit the remote fart button when someone attractive walks past. This is also a fun one when on a conference call with multiple people talking. Hit the fart noise and see if the conversation pauses for a second while everyone tries to figure out who on the call just farted.
2. Depending on the quality of the keyboard, pull a few keys off and swap them with other keys. Or put a piece of tape over the laser on the bottom of the mouse.
3. If they have a wireless mouse, swap the dongle with another one. They will try to use it, and as you sit across from them, you can move it in other directions.
4. I'm sure everyone has seen Internet pictures of people getting their offices and desks trashed when someone goes on vacation. Come up with one of your own, like wrapping everything in plastic wrap, filling the office

with balloons, or completely re-arranging the office in an awkward way.

Parking Lot Pranks:

1. Office pranks don't have to be limited to the inside of the office. Take some honey and stick it under the persons door handle for the next time they open the door.
2. Pick up an inappropriate bumper sticker for their car.
3. If you get your hands on the keys, move the car from one side of the parking lot to the other, then return the keys to their desk. Enjoy the show at the end of the day as they panic about the car.
4. Use the keys to place some more of that smelly fish or food product under the seat, or in the trunk.

Other Pranks:

1. Do you need to dial 9 to get an outside line from your office? Shoot someone a message and ask them to call you on your extension 9911 and see if they figure out where it goes.
2. Is your buddy in the men's room taking a poo? Toss a few things over the stall at him. My suggestion is wadded paper and toilet tissue. Try not to be too mean, you don't want

them to pucker up too much and not be able to finish the job.
3. Do you see your manager walking in your direction while your co-worker doesn't? Just as they walk within hearing distance start saying, "That's kind of mean, I don't think _ is that bad at all."

When it comes to playing office pranks, keep in mind who your audience is. Is this person a friend who can take a joke? And are they the kind of person who might return the favor, and can you take a joke? If the answer is no to either of those questions, you might want to hold off, but if it is yes, then have some fun. With office pranks, keep in mind they are jokes and for the fun of it, they are not intended to get that person in trouble in any way, and they are not intended to get you in trouble either.

Appendix

[i] Gary L. Neilson and Julie Wulf, *"How Many Direct Reports?"* https://hbr.org/2012/04/how-many-direct-reports (April 2012).

[ii] Neil Patel, *"90% Of Startups Fail: Here's What You Need To Know About The 10%"* https://www.forbes.com/sites/neilpatel/2015/01/16/90-of-startups-will-fail-heres-what-you-need-to-know-about-the-10/#2926ce586679 (January 16, 2015).

[iii] Dale Carnegie, *"How to Win Friends and Influence People"* (Simon and Schuster, 1936)

[iv] *"Employers Want Communication Skills in New Hires"* http://www.mba.com/global/the-gmat-blog-hub/the-official-gmat-blog/2014/aug/employers-want-communication-skills-in-new-hires.aspx (August 7, 2014)

[v] Richard Branson, *"Losing My Virginity: How I've Survived, Had Fun, and Made a Fortune Doing Business My Way,"* (Crown Publishing Group, 1998)

[vi] Becoming Warren Buffett, (Kunhardt Films)

[vii] Susan Cain, *"Quiet: The Power of Introverts in a World That Can't Stop Talking,"* (Crown Publishing Group, 2012)

[viii] Tucker: The Man and His Dream, (Paramount Pictures)

[ix] Julie Beck, *"Science Says Doing These Things Will Make You Seem Smarter"* http://www.businessinsider.com/these-things-will-make-you-seem-smarter-2015-1 (January 25, 2015)

[x] Simon Sinek, *"Start with Why: How Great Leaders Inspire Everyone to Take Action,"* (2009)

[xi] Tim Ferriss, *"The 4-Hour Workweek,"* (Crown Publishing Group, 2007)

[xii] Kevin Smith, *Tough Shit: Life Advice from a Fat, Lazy Slob Who Did Good* (Gotham 2012)

[xiii] Carnegie, *"How to Win Friends and Influence People."*

[xiv] *"Employees Who Stay In Companies Longer Than Two Years Get Paid 50% Less"* https://www.forbes.com/sites/cameronkeng/2014/06/22/employees-that-stay-in-companies-longer-than-2-years-get-paid-50-less/#455a208fe07f, (June 2014)

[xv] B.F. Skinner (1904 -1990) is a behavioral psychologist who developed the theory of operant conditioning, in which behavior followed by positive reinforcement results in an increased probability of that behavior occurring in the future.

Printed in Great Britain
by Amazon